The Economics of Human Rights

Ruud Bronkhorst

The Economics of Human Rights

Using the Living Income/Fair Price Approach to Combat Poverty

palgrave
macmillan

Ruud Bronkhorst
InfoBridge Foundation
Nijmegen, The Netherlands

ISBN 978-3-030-59165-6 ISBN 978-3-030-59166-3 (eBook)
https://doi.org/10.1007/978-3-030-59166-3

This Palgrave Macmillan imprint is published by the registered company Springer Nature Switzerland AG.
The registered company address is: Gewerbestrasse 11, 6330 Cham, Switzerland

To Johanna

Preface

This book is the result of a long search for an answer to the question of how a 'fair' producer price should be determined.

It started with a control mission for the Dutch Association of World Shops (DAWS) in India in 2004. World Shops promised a lot to their customers, such as better working conditions and no discrimination, but also the payment of fair prices to the producers and fair wages to the workers. Therefore, one of my objectives was to find out whether this happened in reality. On the whole I was quite satisfied with the working conditions in companies in India that sold their produce through the World Shops, but it also became clear that there existed no uniform definition of the meaning of 'fair.' This resulted in my first article published on this subject, in *Economic and Political Weekly* (Bronkhorst 2004).

In 2005 I was in Burkina Faso to study the effects of structural food aid. At that time the World Food Programme (WFP) was involved in local purchase of grains. Grain was bought in one district of the country to be distributed in another part of the country where there was a lack of food. This was a very positive and important development from the period in that all food aid was imported, which was still the case when I was working with WFP in the 1980s. In addition to problems farmers faced with late payments, there was also the problem that the market price the farmers were paid was insufficient. Hence, the question arose: What price should be paid to the farmers for their products to assure them of a decent income?

This question has led me to research the question: How to define and calculate a Fair Price?

This book is devoted to that search and the answers I have found to date.

Over the years I have published several articles and discussion papers about the subject of fair prices (see literature list). I have also discussed the approach at different forums and conferences. I am very grateful for all comments received. In this book I make use of the ideas developed in those articles and discussions and advance them further. Therefore some parts have been copied from these own publications, especially Bronkhorst (2004, 2016, 2018 and 2019). Among the many people whose comments I have profited from I want to mention especially Eberhard Krain, Linnert Steffens, Marc Bleijenberg, Johanna van der Spek and Sandra van Hulsen. Further I am grateful to Joy Manne, Elly van Roest, Ruud Crul, Hanneke Burger and Peter Jansen for reading the whole manuscript or parts of it, and for their comments. I am grateful to my colleagues at InfoBridge Foundation for their support.

A special thanks to all workers and peasants I interviewed during the years who shared their thoughts and grievances with me.

GIZ and SOMO kindly allowed me to make use of their research. Thanks also to Karel Dekker for his advice on Annex III. Of course, I alone am responsible for any mistakes.

Not everyone will agree with my conclusions, but I will be satisfied when this book inspires others to work on this interesting and important question and proceed with this work.

Zwolle, The Netherlands
June 2020

Ruud Bronkhorst

References

Bronkhorst, Ruud (2004): "Fair' prices and wages'", *Economic and Political Weekly* vol. XXXIX no. 34, August 21–27, 2004. https://www.epw.in/journal/2004/34/commentary/fair-prices-and-wages.html.

Bronkhorst, Ruud (2016): 'Guide How to Calculate Fair Prices', InfoBridge, 2016. https://www.researchgate.net/publication/310133756_Guide_How_To_Calculate_Fair_Prices.

Bronkhorst, Ruud (2018): 'Fair Prices to achieve a Living Income for Small Farmers and its relation to local food purchase programs', *Sociology and Anthropology*, December 3, 2018 http://www.hrpub.org/journals/article_info.php?aid=7538.

Bronkhorst, Ruud (2019): 'Fair Producer Prices', *Conference paper AES* (Agricultural Economics Society) Annual Conference 2019. https://www.researchgate.net/publication/332727083_Fair_Producer_Prices_AES.

Contents

Abbreviations

AFWA	Asia Floor Wage Alliance
BF	Burkina Faso
CAP	Common Agricultural Policy
CFAF	Franc CFA, the currency used in West Africa
CIC/B	Comité Interprofessionnelle sur les Céréales Burkina
CSR	Corporate Social Responsibility
CT	Cash transfer
DAWS	Dutch Association of World Shops
EEC	European Economic Community
ETI	Ethical Trading Initiative
EU	European Union
FAO	Food and Agriculture Organization
FAOBF	Food and Agriculture Organization Burkina Faso
FCFA	West African CFA franc
FP	Fair Price
FPGs	Fair Price Goals
FWF	Fair Wear
GLA	Greater London Authority
Ha	Hectare
HH	Household
ICN	India Committee of Netherlands
IFPI	International Food Policy Research Institute
ILO	International Labour Organization
INTERFAIS	International Food Aid Information System
INSD	Institut National de la Statistique et de la Démographie
IPCC	Intergovernmental Panel on Climate Change
Kg	Kilogram

KHR	Cambodian riel
LCA	Low cost but acceptable
LI	Living Income
LW	Living Wage
MARH	Ministère de l'Agriculture, de l'Hydraulique et des Ressources Halieutiques du Burkina Faso
MIS	Minimum Income Standards
MKW	Malawi kwacha
NGO	Non-Governmental Organization
OECD	Organisation for Economic Co-operation and Development
OPM	Oxford Policy Management
P4P	Purchase for Progress
PPP	Purchasing Power Parity
Rs	Indian Rupees
SAI	Social Accountability International
SARPN	Southern African Regional Poverty Network
UNDP	United Nations Development Programme
UP	Unité de Production (Production Unit)
WB	World Bank
WFP	World Food Programme
WHO	World Health Organization

List of Figures

List of Tables

List of Boxes

Introduction

This book is an introduction to the Living Income/Fair Price approach. Since a large part of the world's working population is underpaid, and therefore does not have enough income to feed themselves and their family in a decent way, there is a need for another approach to producer prices than the usual neo-classical approach with its emphasis on market and equilibrium prices. This is why the Living Income/Fair Price methodology, explained in this book, has been developed. The Living Income/Fair Price theory is a price theory based on ethics. Ethical here implies that it is based on Universal Human Rights.

Many interventions are needed in order to achieve a society in which everybody earns at least the minimum for an adequate standard of living. It is important that all these measures are in line with one another. There is no silver bullet to solve all problems. Not only are many measures needed, they must also be coordinated. It is impossible to outline a single theory that fits all. Each case is different and needs a different approach. This makes a 'holistic' approach necessary. Each approach has to be critically re-examined from time to time.

In this book the focus will be on a single item that has been neglected too much so far: a 'Fair' producer price. Without a minimum that a producer receives for his/her product, it is impossible to continue production. Fair prices are not the solution to all the producers' problems. Many other interventions are needed as well, but a decent income gives the producer the possibility to make choices for him/herself. But what is the minimum that producers and workers should receive, and how can this be calculated? This book presents an approach to determine this minimum price the producer should receive. This will be done using the concepts of Living Wage (LW) and Living Income (LI). These concepts indicate the minimum people should earn from their work. Based on these concepts, so-called Fair Prices can be calculated.

The book is divided into two parts. The first section is an introduction to the basic questions regarding why a separate theory for producer prices is needed. The UN Universal Declaration of Human Rights and the subsequent Sustainable Development Goals (SDGs) and their practical consequences in the form of Living Wage (LW) and Living Income (LI) are discussed. In order to achieve living wages and incomes it is essential that the prevalent view of market prices as the logical result of a well-functioning market system is called into question. Equilibrium prices only exist in a situation of perfect market conditions, a situation that rarely exists in reality. Along with market-disturbing elements like monopolies and oligopolies, there is also the fact that the demands of the poorest parts of the population are not taken into consideration because they are not reflected in the effective demand.

An alternative is proposed, namely, 'Fair' Prices (FP). After an explanation of how Fair Wages can be calculated, the effects of the payment of Fair and Living Wages and Fair Prices to the producers as well as third parties are discussed.

Part I starts with a discussion about the meaning of the word 'fair,' both now and in the past. Then we show how the Universal Declaration of Human Rights and its follow-up the 'Sustainable Development Goals' (SDGs) are developed into the concepts of Living Wage and Living Income. Living Wage and Living Income play an important role in the rest of the book, being the concepts that Fair Prices are based upon. After an explanation of how to calculate Fair Wages, applied to a case in India, the effects of the payment of fair wages and fair prices based on poverty lines on socio-economic development are discussed, both economic and social.

Part II is devoted to agriculture and especially to the problem how to calculate a Fair Price for each different agricultural product. The methodology how to calculate fair prices for agricultural products is explained, both theoretically and in the form of case studies. Attention is given to the socio-economic effects of the payment of fair prices to producers, on both producers and consumers, and on the community and the region as well. The roles of governments, NGOs and companies are also discussed.

The effects of the payment of fair prices on child labour, the environment and climate change are analysed separately. Subsequently also the case of export products receives attention.

A methodology is introduced to determine the price for each agricultural product in order to enable the farmer to achieve a living income. Because this price is based on human rights instead of on the market, a paradigm change in our thinking about prices is required.

A distinction is made between 'Fair Prices' when the farmer is employed full-time and 'Not-fully employed prices' where time is available for other income-generating activities as well. Case studies from Malawi, Burkina Faso, Cote d'Ivoire and Cambodia show how these prices can be calculated in practice.

Readers who are mainly interested in the methodology of how to calculate Fair Prices for agricultural products may want to skip Part I and go directly to Part II.

Although primarily meant for (development) economists and sociologists, both experts and students, the book is also meant to stimulate discussion among everyone involved in agricultural policies, both in developing and developed countries. It provides new insights on how to combine economic theory and ethics, and how to formulate policies to combat the roots of poverty. For farmers it shows how minimum prices for each of their products can be calculated. The use of these calculations can serve during their price negotiations.

PART I

General

CHAPTER 1

What Is 'Fair': Different Opinions

Abstract There are a lot of possible ways to interpret 'fair'. Should 'fair' prices and wages be paid because of their economic or social necessity, moral value or as a charity? Does the worker have a moral or economic 'right' to a fair remuneration or is it something we grant him or her because of our 'goodness'?

Thinking about 'fair' prices and wages, though not always under that name, has been going on for a very long time. When the idea of a divine world in which the structure of the whole society was fixed weakened, philosophers also began to think about moral issues.

After a period in which the 'natural' and the 'market price' of labour and 'exchange value' and 'use value' of products were central to the discussions, the neo-classical school replaced the classical concept with an analysis of the equilibrium of supply and demand in a stationary state. They based a theory of the relative prices of commodities on the concept of utility.

What is proposed in this book is to include universal human rights as a determining factor in the determination of market prices.

Keywords Fair • Adam Smith • Utility • John Stuart Mill

R. Bronkhorst, *The Economics of Human Rights*,
https://doi.org/10.1007/978-3-030-59166-3_1

There are a lot of possible ways to interpret 'fair.' Should 'fair' prices and wages be paid because it is an economic or social necessity, a moral value or as a charity? Does the worker have a moral or economic 'right' to a fair remuneration or is it something we grant him or her because of our 'goodness'? Is it 'fair' that you get paid more because you have had the opportunity to study, in contrast to a person who didn't have the opportunity for education because he/she was born in the wrong place, in the wrong society, in the wrong family?

Large parts of the population have too little income because the prices fetched for their products are not sufficient to live on, such as in the case of many artisans, small farmers, and so on.

Thinking about 'fair' prices and wages, though not always under that name, has been going on for a very long time. With the weakening of the idea of a divine world in which the structure of the whole society was fixed, philosophers also began to think about moral issues. Adam Smith (1723–1790), famous for the so-called invisible hand, wrote in his best-known work *The Wealth of Nations*, "No society can surely be flourishing and happy, of which the far greater part of the members are poor and miserable. It is but equity, besides, that they who feed, clothe and lodge the whole body of the people should have such a share of the produce of their own labour as to be themselves tolerably well fed, clothed and lodged" (Smith). After a period in which the 'natural' price and the 'market price' of labour and the 'exchange value' and 'use value' of products were central to the discussions, the neo-classical school replaced the classical concept with an analysis of the equilibrium of supply and demand in a stationary state. They based a theory of the relative prices of commodities on the concept of utility. The price of a commodity is governed by its marginal utility, not by its usefulness.[1] John Stuart Mill (1806–1873) writes in his "Greatest Happiness Principle" that "Utility should be maximized by focusing on the general net happiness in society, calculated according to both quantities and qualities" (Wright). Walras further developed the marginalist approach by describing the economic system in general mathematical terms.

Economics became more and more a mathematical instead of a moral science.

[1] The Penguin Dictionary of Economics defines Marginal Utility as follows: The extra satisfaction gained by a consumer from a small increment in the consumption of a commodity (Penguin Dictionary of Economics, 6th edition). So this can be different from useful.

This has again provoked a reaction, power structures are analysed again and the concept of 'fair' trade has become more important, but the mainstream notion is still always that economics is more a mathematical than a social science. 'Fair' is still never the centre of attention in theory development.

Annex A provides a short overview of thinking about the concept of 'Fair' by economists.

An interesting question that arises when discussing underpayment is where to draw the line between exploitation and a reasonable share of benefits. In this book I will try to sketch the outlines of a system that takes into account the minimum benefits workers should reap from their work, without delving into the philosophical question of how to define economic justice. Here we try to develop a practical approach to put into practice the minimum standards that should be applied according to the 'Universal Declaration of Human Rights.'

What is proposed in this book is to include universal human rights as a determining factor in the determination of market prices. Market prices are dependent on many external factors and do not appear as if by magic on the market. Governments place many rules and restrictions on the functioning of markets. By including universal human rights, marginal costs are redefined to include living wages and living incomes. Now in many countries production and marginal costs already include legal minimum wages. Where these minimum wages are equal or higher than living wages, nothing changes. Only in those cases where minimum wages are below living wages (we come back to the calculation of living wages in the following chapters), total costs for the producer will change. This step to the inclusion of living wages instead of minimum wages is not so large, but the inclusion of living incomes is something quite new. This will be discussed in Part II of the book.

CHAPTER 2

Ethics: Human Rights and Basic Needs

Abstract Universal Human Rights, Articles 23 and 25 are especially relevant to the matters of living wages and incomes and the corresponding fair prices. These articles are at the base of the SDGs, the Sustainable Development Goals, adopted in 2015 by the United Nations.

The concepts of Living Wage and Living Income that are used in this book are based on these two UN articles, as is the 'Living Income/Fair Price' methodology explained in this book.

In order to put these concepts into practice, a paradigm change from the use of prices decided by the market with all its imperfections to an approach founded on ethics is needed. 'Ethical' here implies that any worker receives a decent income for full-time, sustainable work.

Keywords Ethics • Human rights • Basic needs • Universal Human Rights • Article 23 and 25 • SDGs • Living Wage • Living Income • 'Living Income/Fair Price' methodology • Ethical

When we refer to Universal Human Rights, Articles 23 and 25 are especially relevant to the matters of living wages and incomes and the corresponding fair prices. These articles state the following:

Article 23

"Everyone who works has the right to just and favourable remuneration ensuring for himself and his family an existence worthy of human

R. Bronkhorst, *The Economics of Human Rights*,
https://doi.org/10.1007/978-3-030-59166-3_2

dignity, and supplemented, if necessary, by other means of social protection."

Article 25

"Everyone has the right to a standard of living adequate for the health and well-being of himself and of his family, including food, clothing, housing and medical care and necessary social services, and the right to security in the event of unemployment, sickness, disability, widowhood, old age or other lack of livelihood in circumstances beyond his control."[1]

These articles are at the base of the SDGs, the Sustainable Development Goals, adopted in 2015 by the United Nations.

Goal 1, 'No Poverty' and Goal 2, 'Zero Hunger' are about ending poverty and hunger, and achieving food security.

"Goal 1: End poverty in all its forms everywhere

Extreme poverty rates have been cut by more than half since 1990. While this is a remarkable achievement, one in five people in developing regions still live on less than $1.90 a day, and there are millions more who make little more than this daily amount, plus many people risk slipping back into poverty.

Poverty is more than the lack of income and resources to ensure a sustainable livelihood. Its manifestations include hunger and malnutrition, limited access to education and other basic services, social discrimination and exclusion as well as the lack of participation in decision-making. Economic growth must be inclusive to provide sustainable jobs and promote equality."

"Goal 2: End hunger, achieve food security and improved nutrition and promote sustainable agriculture

It is time to rethink how we grow, share and consume our food.

If done right, agriculture, forestry and fisheries can provide nutritious food for all and generate decent incomes, while supporting people-centred rural development and protecting the environment.

Right now, our soils, freshwater, oceans, forests and biodiversity are being rapidly degraded. Climate change is putting even more pressure on the resources we depend on, increasing risks associated with disasters such as droughts and floods. Many rural women and men can no longer make ends meet on their land, forcing them to migrate to cities in search of opportunities.

[1] Source: http://www.un.org/en/universal-declaration-human-rights/.

A profound change of the global food and agriculture system is needed if we are to nourish today's 815 million hungry and the additional 2 billion people expected by 2050.

The food and agriculture sector offers key solutions for development, and is central for hunger and poverty eradication."[2]

A recent report of IPCC, "Land is a Critical Resource", sets out options to tackle land degradation, and prevent or adapt to further climate change (IPCC) (see also Part II, Ch. 22 under *Fair Prices and Other Development Issues*).

The concepts of Living Wage and Living Income that are used in this book are based on these two UN articles, as is the 'Living Income/Fair Price' methodology explained here.

In order to put these concepts into practice, what is needed is a paradigm change from the use of prices decided by the market with all its imperfections to an approach founded on ethics. I will come back to this later. 'Ethical' here implies that any worker receives a decent income for full-time, sustainable work.

[2] Source Goal 1 and Goal 2: http://www.un.org/sustainabledevelopment/hunger/.

CHAPTER 3

Concepts Derived from the Human Rights: Living Wage and Living Income

Abstract An 'ethical' or 'human rights based' approach implies that every worker, whether wage earner or independent farmer, earns enough to sustain his/her household. For workers this implies at least a 'living wage'. In reality however, a number of minimum wages exist, that may be higher or lower than the living wage needed, such as the legal minimum wage and the prevailing wage

About the definition and way of calculation of Living Wage, there is no universal agreement. Different definitions of living wage are used. Two major different ways of arriving at a living wage are the negotiated approach and the calculated approach using a formula, among which is the 1998 ETI Living Wage Summit formula.

In 2013, a definition of a living wage was agreed to by the Global Living Wage Coalition. This has been worked out in the standard work on living wages by Richard and Martha Anker *Living Wages Around the World: Manual for Measurement*, whereby "Living costs are divided into three categories: food, housing, and other essential needs."

For Living Income a definition was proposed during a Practitioners' Workshop in 2015, hosted by ISEAL and GIZ: "A living income is the net income of a household earned/generated under conditions of decent work, sufficient to enable all members of the (average) household to afford a decent standard of living."

R. Bronkhorst, *The Economics of Human Rights*,
https://doi.org/10.1007/978-3-030-59166-3_3

The definition used for Living Income in this book is an extension of this definition from 2015. The extension implies that added to this is a percentage to enable additional investments to improve future yields.

Keywords ILO • Living Wage • Calculation • Benchmark • ETI • SA8000 • Household • Family • UK • USA • Global Living Wage Coalition • Living Income • ISEAL

Although there is no international labour convention on living wages (Vaughan-Whitehead), the ILO has made clear references to it, from 1919 in the Constitution of ILO onwards, and has included living wage as a human right in several major Declarations (Anker 2011).

In June 2008 an ILO Declaration on Social Justice was adopted by The International Labour Conference that supports "policies in regard to wages and earnings, hours and other conditions of work, designed to ensure a just share of the fruits of progress to all and a ***minimum living wage*** to all employed and in need of such protection" (my italics).

There is no universal agreement about the definition and method of calculation of Living Wage.

Different definitions of living wage that are used:

> Clary, for instance, has defined the Living Wage as "a wage equivalent to the poverty line for a family of four, or the amount of income generated by such a wage that would allow such a family to secure the food, shelter, clothing, health care, transportation, and other necessities of living in modern society." (Clary, cited in Werner and Lim, 436).

ETI defines in 'Base code clause 5: Living wages are paid'

5.1 Wages and benefits paid for a standard working week meet, at a minimum, national legal standards or industry benchmark standards, whichever is higher. In any event wages should always be enough to meet basic needs and to provide some discretionary income.

The *Fair Wear Foundation* (FWF) states:

> A living wage should cover "basic needs and some discretionary income," according to FWF's Code of Labour Practices. So (how) can that be

> translated into an exact number? There are a variety of approaches to answering this question, many of them including complicated formulas and interesting discussions about what should and shouldn't be counted as 'basic needs.' FWF's wage ladder was designed to help workers, factory managers, and brands in the process of setting target wage levels in factories and beyond. (FWF)

According to Werner and Lim, we find in the literature three approaches to 'calculating' the Living Wage.

First, workers negotiate a Living Wage themselves with their employers.

Second, a Living Wage may be determined using a 'relative' benchmark. Suggested relative benchmarks include a percentage of median earnings or a multiple percentage of the poverty threshold. This approach is not often used.

Third, the Living Wage rate is calculated with reference to an 'absolute' benchmark, that is, the use of a basket of essential goods and services that a household needs to ensure a basic standard of living, taking into account regional variations regarding the cost of these needs (Werner and Lim).

In practice, two major different ways of arriving at a living wage are discussed in the literature. These are the negotiated approach and the calculated approach using a formula. A mixture of both approaches is found as well.

The negotiated approach implies negotiations between workers (unions) and management whereby the workers themselves decide what they consider a living wage. Not surprisingly, many proponents of the negotiated approach are to be found within the ILO. The ILO considers two factors very important when looking at minimum wages, namely (a) that the level of a minimum wage should be set high enough to be considered decent and (b) that social partners should be involved, not only in the design and monitoring of the minimum wage system, but also in the decision-making related to setting the level of the minimum wage (ILO Global Wage Report 2008/09). This implies a negotiated approach with a decent wage as minimum.

The calculated approach involves the use of a formula to calculate a living wage.

ETI

In the *Ethical Trading Initiative (ETI) 1998 Living wage formula* a living wage is to be earned over a maximum working week of 48 hours and basic needs are defined as housing, energy, nutrition, clothing, health care, education, potable water, childcare, transportation and savings, though the possibility of including further need categories (e.g. entertainment, vacation, paid family leave, retirement, life insurance and personal liability insurance) is floated (Steele).

The present ETI Base code states: "Wages and benefits paid for a standard working week meet, at a minimum, national legal standards or industry benchmark standards, whichever is higher. In any event wages should always be enough to meet basic needs and to provide some discretionary income" (ETI Base code).

Steele suggested the *1998 ETI Living Wage Summit formula*. Interestingly, this formula can no longer be found on the actual ETI website, suggesting that ETI does not want to be associated with it, but there is no indication of the reasons.

The 1998 ETI Living Wage Summit formula

This formula calculates the living wage from the cost of basic needs per person, multiplied by average household size, then divided by the average number of earners per household, with an allowance for savings added on (Steele):

$$\frac{\text{Average household size} \times \text{cost of basic needs per person}}{\text{Average number of adult earners per household}} + \text{savings}\left(\text{set at } 10\% \text{ of income}\right)$$

SA8000

SA8000[1]: "A 'living wage' means one that enables workers, for their labor during a standard workweek, to support half the basic needs of an average-sized family, based on local prices near the workplace" and "A company shall pay a living wage for a standard work week (i.e., no more than 48 hours per week or less if set at a lower level by national law) and workers shall earn that sum without working overtime. Basic needs include essential expenses such as food, clean water, clothes, shelter, transport, education and a discretionary income, as well as the workers' costs for legally required social benefits (e.g. health care, medical insurance, unemployment insurance, retirement plan, etc.)" (SA8000).

While *1998 ETI Living Wage Summit formula* refers to household size and adult earners per household, SA8000 mentions family size. Although often considered the same, there may be differences between these concepts. A household may consist of more than one family.

These formulas do not take into account provisions provided by the employer, such as free housing, medical insurance or retirement schemes. These provisions should be calculated though, and may be deducted from the calculated Living Wage of the workers involved.

It is possible to combine these formulas into the following formula:

$$\frac{\text{Average household size} \times (\text{cost of food} + \text{cost of non food per person})}{\text{Average number of adult earners per household}} + \text{savings}(\text{set at } 10\% \text{ of income})$$

Whereby:

- The local average household size (which can be different from a standard family) and the average number of adult earners per household are used;
- The sum of the weights of its members is calculated by valuing adults as 1 and persons aged under 18 as 0.5;

[1] Social Accountability International (SAI) is a non-governmental, multi-stakeholder organization whose mission is to advance the human rights of workers around the world.

- For the adult earners both men and women are calculated as 1.[2] Children between 16 and 18 years may be calculated as 0.5;[3]
- Where the non-food component cannot easily be determined, the extrapolated approach with percentages adapted to local circumstances can be used;
- For the food component a norm of 2400 kcal/day could be used;
- Deduct all provisions provided.

[2] Productivity of men and women in agriculture can be different, as is the case between two people of the same sex. In this approach, the Living Wage that people should earn is independent of their productivity. What counts here is that everyone who works full time should earn a Living Wage at least.

[3] It is usual everywhere that children during peak periods work with their parents on the farm, during their school holidays, after school hours and so on. Therefore they cannot be left out, but cannot be valued as adult full-time workers either. Note that child work is acceptable within the limits of the ILO core conventions only. See Minimum Age (Agriculture) Convention, 1921 (No. 10), update R146—Minimum Age Recommendation, 1973 (No. 146)

Minimum Age (Agriculture) Convention, 1921 (No. 10)

Article 1

Children under the age of fourteen years may not be employed or work in any public or private agricultural undertaking, or in any branch thereof, save outside the hours fixed for school attendance. If they are employed outside the hours of school attendance, the employment shall not be such as to prejudice their attendance at school.

Article 2

For purposes of practical vocational instruction the periods and the hours of school attendance may be so arranged as to permit the employment of children on light agricultural work and in particular on light work connected with the harvest, provided that such employment shall not reduce the total annual period of school attendance to less than eight months.

ILO R146—Minimum Age Recommendation, 1973 (No. 146)

7.

(a) Members should take as their objective the progressive raising to 16 years of the minimum age for admission to employment or work specified in pursuance of Article 2 of the Minimum Age Convention, 1973.

(b) Where the minimum age for employment or work covered by Article 2 of the Minimum Age Convention, 1973, is still below 15 years, urgent steps should be taken to raise it to that level.

8. Where it is not immediately feasible to fix a minimum age for all employment in agriculture and in related activities in rural areas, a minimum age should be fixed at least for employment on plantations and in the other agricultural undertakings.

To determine the food basket different approaches use different calculations for the kcal/day, ranging from 2100 to 3000 kcal/day. The World Health Organization (WHO) has developed guidelines on the average calorie supply of workers in the least developed countries needed to perform a full day of medium-heavy work: 2400/kcal/day. For heavy physical work this can be raised (see a list prepared by FAO for energy costs of activities) (Joint FAO/WHO/UNU Expert Consultation on Human Energy Requirements Annex 5: Energy costs of activities).

Living Wage Studies in UK and USA

UK

In the UK there are two different living wages, one for Greater London and another for the rest of the UK.

According to Pennycook and Lawton, at the core of both living wage rates is an estimate of the costs of a socially acceptable minimum standard of living for a range of household types, although these costs are calculated in different ways for each rate. The London living wage rate is based on a 'basic living costs' approach which seeks to estimate a 'low cost but acceptable' (LCA) budget for 14 different household types in the capital. This LCA budget is made up of housing, council tax, transport, childcare and all other costs in 'a regular shopping basket.' An average wage is then calculated that would meet the costs of this budget for different family types, with the average weighted to reflect the composition of families in London. For 2012 the GLA (Greater London Authority) living wage unit estimated the wage needed to meet their LCA budget to be £7.10 per hour. The GLA then calculates the wage that would be required to lift a worker and their family above the capital's *relative* poverty threshold of 60% of median household income. This produces a wage rate of £7.80 in 2012 (GLA Economics 2012). An average is then taken of the 'basic living costs' wage and the 'income distribution' wage to calculate a 'poverty threshold wage' (£7.45 in 2012). A 15% margin is then added to account for any unforeseen events that would otherwise take a family below the minimum standard of living. This took the 2012 rate to £8.55 per hour.

The UK living wage is calculated using a similar approach to the LCA budget calculation, but draws instead on the Minimum Income Standards (MIS) project based at the University of Loughborough and supported by the Joseph Rowntree Foundation. The MIS uses focus groups to agree a minimum acceptable family budget for nine different household types. It therefore reflects prevailing social norms rather than expert opinion (Hirsch, 2011 in Pennycook and Lawton).

US Living Wage Calculator

Geographically specific expenditure data are collected that are related to a family's likely minimum costs of food, childcare, health insurance, housing, transportation and other basic necessities (e.g. clothing, personal care items). On basis of these cost elements and the rough effects of income and payroll taxes, the minimum employment earnings necessary to meet a family's basic needs while also maintaining self-sufficiency are determined.

For housing it is assumed that a one-adult family would rent a single-occupancy unit (zero bedrooms) for an individual adult household, that a two-adult family would rent a one-bedroom apartment, and that two-adult-and-one-or-two-child families would rent a two-bedroom apartment. Families with three children would rent a three bedroom apartment (the adults are allocated one bedroom and the children two bedrooms).

Nadeau and Glasmeier admit that the living wage model is a 'step up' from poverty as measured by the poverty thresholds but it is a small step up, one that accounts for only the basic needs of a family (Nadeau and Glasmeier).

In 2013 the following definition of a living wage was agreed to by the Global Living Wage Coalition, consisting of Fairtrade International, Forest Stewardship Council (FSC), GoodWeave, Sustainable Agriculture Network/Rainforest Alliance (SAN/RA), Social Accountability International (SAI) and UTZ Certified.

> *A living wage is*:
>
> The remuneration received for a standard work week by a worker in a particular place sufficient to afford a decent standard of living for the worker and her or his family. Elements of a decent standard of living include food, water, housing, education, health care, transport, clothing, and other essential needs including provision for unexpected events. (Global Living Wage Coalition, 2013)

The OECD Guidelines for Multinational Enterprises, 2011, state that: "when multinational enterprises operate in developing countries, where comparable employers may not exist, (they should) provide the best possible wages, benefits and conditions of work, within the framework of government policies. These should be related to the economic position of the enterprise but should be at least adequate to satisfy the basic needs of the workers and their families" (OECD 2011).

The standard work on Living Wages by Richard and Martha Anker, *Living Wages Around the World: Manual for Measurement*, states: "Estimating a living wage begins by estimating the cost of a basic but decent life style for a worker and his/her family. This involves adding up the cost of three expenditure groups: food (for a low-cost nutritious diet), housing (for basic healthy housing), and other essential expenses for a family, and then adding a small margin for sustainability and emergencies" (Anker and Anker 2017). When this cost of a basic but decent life for a family is divided by the number of full-time workers per family, the outcome is the Net Living Wage. Anker uses "labor force participation rates for persons 25–59 to estimate the number of full-time equivalent workers per couple" (Anker and Anker 2017). In their approach living costs are divided into three categories: food, housing and other essential needs. Food costs are estimated based on: (i) a low-cost nutritious diet that meets World Health Organization (WHO) recommendations on calories, macronutrients and micronutrients and is consistent with local food preferences and a country's development level and (ii) local food prices for the types, qualities and quantities of foods that workers typically buy. Housing costs are estimated using international (UN-HABITAT) and national standards for decency. Cost of other essential needs is estimated using an extrapolation method based on secondary household expenditure data. This is then "post checked" to make sure that sufficient funds are included for health care, education and transportation.

The Anker approach is important because it has been accepted by major organizations, organized in the Global Living Wage Coalition. They write on their website about Anker Estimating the Cost of a Basic but Decent Lifestyle for Workers and Families:

"Living costs are divided into three categories: food, housing, and other essential needs."

- Food costs are estimated based on: (i) a low cost nutritious diet that meets World Health Organization (WHO) recommendations on calories, macronutrients, and micronutrients and is consistent with local food preferences and a country's development level; and (ii) local food prices for the types, qualities, and quantities of foods that workers typically buy based on new data collection that involves workers and key informants. This approach to the model diet uses a more stringent nutrition standard than the typical approach at present, which ensures only a sufficient number of calories. By collecting local food prices with worker input, realistic food prices are obtained that mimic workers' food shopping habits and preferences.

- Housing costs are estimated using international (UN-HABITAT) and national standards for decency (e.g. dwellings located outside slums and unsafe areas that have permanent walls, roofs that do not leak, and adequate ventilation; amenities such as electricity, water, and sanitary toilet facilities; and sufficient living space so parents can sleep separately from children). The cost of acceptable housing is based on visits to local housing with workers.
- Lastly for practical reasons, cost of other essential needs is estimated using an extrapolation method based on secondary household expenditure data. This is then "post checked" to make sure that sufficient funds are included for health care, education, and transportation. This guards against the extrapolation method replicating poor living conditions as it is based on currently observed expenditure according to available household expenditure data.

Total cost per capita of a basic but decent standard of living is then scaled up to arrive at a cost for a typical family size in the area. A small margin is then added to provide for unexpected events and emergencies such as illnesses and accidents, to help ensure sustainability and avoid the perpetual poverty trap. To arrive at the living wage estimate, the estimated total cost of a decent standard of living for a typical family is then defrayed over the typical number of full-time-equivalent workers per family for that location.

This methodology is a practical compromise between separately estimating the cost of each and every expense families have and the most common approach currently used for estimating living wage in developing countries, which uses just two expense groups (food costs based on a model diet and non-food costs based on secondary data). Using normative standards for decent housing and estimating housing costs separately (not as part of non-food costs, as in typical methodologies) ensures that living wage estimates enable workers to afford decent housing. In contrast, typical methodologies rely on available expenditure data to estimate housing costs and thus replicate current (often substandard) housing conditions. Our methodology also better allows for different living wage estimates for rural and urban areas, as housing costs are usually the most important cause of differences in living costs. Our methodology also increases transparency, because the size of the "all other essential costs bucket is much smaller and examined more thoroughly (and adjusted when necessary) than in typical approaches."[4]

There are other approaches than that taken by the Ankers. In the Burkina Faso study in Part II both men and women between the ages of 18 and 60 are valued as 1, and persons from 16 to 18 years as 0.5.

According to Krain and Steffens, authors of the *Handbook to Determine Reference Prices for Agricultural Commodities Based on Benchmarks*, "...while the Ankers Living Income Line functions as a *dignity* benchmark, we consider the WB Poverty Line to be a *survival* benchmark" and "...we have come to the conclusion to use and advocate the Ankers methodology as our most important reference tool—and thus the Ankers living income benchmark as our 'gold standard.' If we use other benchmarks, this is so due to limited time and financial means. We consider the WB Poverty Line to be the second best alternative and advocate the use of national poverty lines, if available" (Krain and Steffens).

The concept of a living wage applies to paid workers only. For agriculturalists who are working on their own account, whether they sell on the market or to large companies, as in the case of cocoa, coffee and tea, another concept had to be developed. This new concept is 'Living Income.'

A Definition for Living Income proposed during a Practitioners' Workshop hosted by ISEAL and GIZ on February 2 and 3, 2015, Eschborn, is as follows:

"A *living income* is the net income of a household earned/generated under conditions of decent work, sufficient to enable all members of the (average) household to afford a decent standard of living," whereby

- Net income = Total income minus all costs.
- Household is a group of people (often family) who form an economic unit (pooling income and other livelihood assets), often (but not always) living under the same roof or within the same compound.
- ILO defines decent work as follows: "Decent work sums up the aspirations of people in their working lives. It involves opportunities for work that is productive and delivers a fair income, security in the

[4] Source: https://www.globallivingwage.org/about/anker-methodology/.

workplace and social protection for families, better prospects for personal development and social integration, freedom for people to express their concerns, organize and participate in the decisions that affect their lives and equality of opportunity and treatment for all women and men."[5]

- FAO defines decent employment as "work that provides a living income and reasonable working conditions. Work should be remunerative and dignified. It should enable people—whether through self-employment or wage labour—to provide for themselves and their families. Workers should be able to perform their work under safe and healthy conditions and have a voice in the work place."[6]

The definition used for Living Income in this book is an extension of this definition from 2015. The extension implies adding to the calculation a percentage to enable additional investments to improve future yields. This percentage might be between 5 and 10 percent, depending on local circumstances. The reason for adding this percentage is that farmers especially need more income to prepare for climate change and soil exhaustion. Extra funds for investments may help them to prepare for the future. This percentage is thus on top of the percentage that is added in the living wage calculations for unexpected events.

It is important to realize that all approaches to living wage and living income take into account the size of the actual family or household. This implies that workers in a region with many small children and large families need a higher living wage than those who are living in areas with fewer small children. The related problem of overly high population growth is not tackled in this approach. We will discuss this further in Part II, Chap. 22 under 'Fair Prices and Other Development Issues'.

We may conclude that an 'ethical' or 'human rights-based' approach implies that every worker, whether wage earner or independent farmer, earns enough to sustain his/her household. For workers this implies at least a 'living wage.' In reality, however, a number of minimum wages exist, which may be higher or lower than the living wage needed, such as the legal minimum wage and the prevailing wage. These will be discussed in the next chapter about Fair Wages.

[5] Source: http://www.ilo.org/global/topics/decent-work/lang%2D%2Den/index.htm.

[6] Source: http://www.fao.org/rural-employment/background/en/.

CHAPTER 4

Fair Wages, What Does It Mean?

Abstract The definition of Vaughan-Whitehead of fair wages is: "Fair wages refer to company practices that lead to sustainable wage developments."

The living wage is the bottom line for a fair wage. The fair wage can be more than the living wage, but never lower, because living wage is only one of the elements of a fair wage.

In order to be able to pay fair wages a number of conditions have to be met, among which is that the living wage must be known, there must be a demand for the product and the consumer must have the financial resources needed to purchase the product. In order to convince employers to pay fair wages to their workers, labour unions can play an important role.

Keywords Fair Wage • Vaughan-Whitehead • Living wage floor • Wage-ladder

In addition to Living Wage, a concept of 'Fair Wage' exists. Vaughan-Whitehead uses two definitions of fair wages, a general definition and an extended definition.

His general definition is "Fair wages refer to 'company practices that lead to sustainable wage developments.'"

R. Bronkhorst, *The Economics of Human Rights*,
https://doi.org/10.1007/978-3-030-59166-3_4

His extended definition is "Fair wages refer to 'Wage levels and wage-fixing mechanisms that provide a living wage floor for workers, while complying with national wage regulations (such as the minimum wage, payment of wages, overtime payments, provision of paid holidays and social insurance payments) ensure proper wage adjustments and lead to balanced wage developments in the company (with regard to wage disparity, skills, individual and collective performance and adequate internal communication and collective bargaining on wage issues)'" (Vaughan-Whitehead, 66).

He proposes in his fair wage approach to integrate the living wage as one but not the only possible criterion for fair wages at company level.

In the so-called Wage Ladder (Figure 1), the minimum wage is the legal minimum wage, while the actual wage is the wage that is actually paid to the workers. The legal minimum wage is often below the living wage, but in some cases it is higher than the living wage, going in the direction of a fair wage. The living wage is the bottom line for a fair wage. The fair wage can be more than the living wage, but never lower, because living wage is one of the elements of a fair wage. This is in line with the approach taken by Vaughan-Whitehead (see below).

An example wage ladder (Fig. 4.1) shows the different layers in wages. Note that the differences are not fixed: the actual wage may be higher than the minimum wage, which may be higher than the living wage and so on. In each situation the ladder will be different.

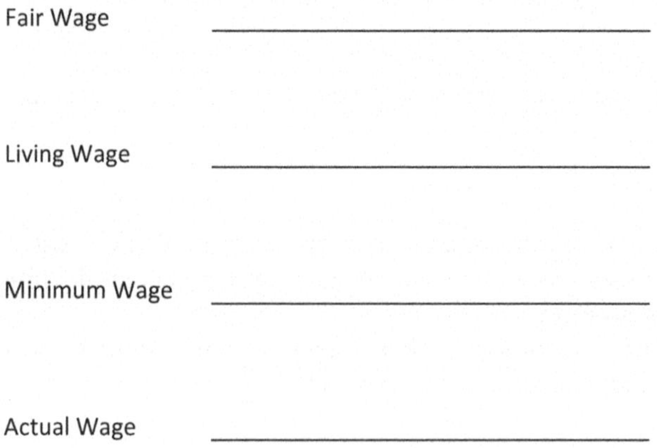

Fig. 4.1 Example Wage Ladder

The difference between the prevailing wages paid and living wages is called the wage gap.

According to Spencer, a fair price is one that has been negotiated through dialogue and transparent price setting and includes an analysis of production and trade costs, a fair wage and a fair profit. A fair wage represents an equitable, negotiated share of the value chain of the product and presumes the payment of at least a living wage (Spencer).

Vaughan-Whitehead proposes a new wage benchmarking approach that contains, along with a general commitment to fair wages, specific benchmarks such as:

- Adherence to local/national law
- Wages should be sufficient to endure minimum living standards
- As far as possible, payment of the average wage prevailing at industry level
- Not imposing a pay system which could be stressful for the workers and adversely affect their health
- Individual labour contract and information on wages
- Distribution of a pay slip specifying the total number of hours worked and distinguishing between payment of normal working hours and payment of overtime
- Collective bargaining with workers' representatives and trade unions are welcome in the enterprise
- Annual increase of nominal wages at least up to the national inflation rate
- Workers' wages related to company performance and thus increase in tandem with better company results. A possible slowdown in wage progression not greater than the slowdown in the company's results
- Higher intensity at work and the acquisition of new skills will be accompanied by proportionate wage increases.

Source: Vaughan-Whitehead table 7.2

A 'fair' wage is at least a living wage, but this wage can only be paid when there is sufficient demand for the product at this price. Not only must demand be present, but consumers must also have the financial resources to purchase. A product may be very useful, and a lot of people might like to have it, but when they lack the necessary financial resources to purchase, the product will fail in the market. Hence, when there is not sufficient demand for a product, neither a 'fair' nor a 'living' wage can be paid and the producer must look for alternative sources of income. Income distribution plays an important role in effective demand.

The payment of a ‘living wage’ usually applies only to the lowest-paid labourers. An interesting question then is how skilled workers will react to a rise in the payment of unskilled and lower-skilled workers to a ‘living wage.’ An effect may be that these workers demand a rise in payment as well. Here we touch on basic philosophical questions such as the rightfulness of differences in income based on the kind of work performed.

Employers are often reluctant to pay living wages to their workers because they have to take into account the survival of the company. History has shown that improvements in wages have often been achieved by labourers who united. Labour unions are very important to achieve stated goals. Not only national labour unions are important but also international cooperation between unions is necessary in order to achieve decent wages everywhere. Cooperation may prevent workers in one country from playing off against workers in another country.

To summarize: in order to be able to pay fair wages a number of conditions have to be met, among which that the living wage must be known,[1] there must be a demand for the product and the consumer must have the financial resources needed to purchase the product. In order to convince employers to pay fair wages to their workers, labour unions can play an important role.

[1] In some cases when the living wage is not known the poverty line can be used, but only where this has been calculated in such a way that the interests of the poorest are also taken into account (see also Chap. 7 about Poverty Lines).

CHAPTER 5

Are Market and Equilibrium Prices and Wages Ethical?

Abstract The income of a producer is determined by the prices received for his products: the sales price.

This sales price should cover all reasonable production costs and at least 'Living Wages' for the producer and all workers involved. These production costs also include transport and distribution costs, depreciation and investment costs.

A sales price is not determined by the producer alone; it is determined on the market by supply and demand. A common mistake is to call these prices equilibrium prices. Equilibrium prices however only exist when there is a situation of perfect market conditions, a situation that rarely exists in reality.

In reality, market prices are **not** equilibrium prices since

1. in reality, there is no perfect competition
2. import and/or export restrictions, or subsidize certain products
3. political interference
4. very important: the demand of the poorest is not taken into account in the equilibrium price

Therefore, a ***paradigm change*** from the use of prices decided by the market with all its imperfections, to an approach founded on ethics is needed. 'Ethical' here is based on Universal Human Rights and implies that any worker receives a decent income for full-time, sustainable work.

R. Bronkhorst, *The Economics of Human Rights*,
https://doi.org/10.1007/978-3-030-59166-3_5

Keywords Equilibrium price • Fair share • Ethical • Monopsonies • Oligopsonies • Demand of the poorest • Paradigm change

The income of a producer is determined by the prices received for his products: the sales price.[1]

This sales price should cover all reasonable production costs and at least 'Living Wages' for the producer and all workers involved. These production costs also include transport and distribution costs, depreciation and investment costs.

A sales price is not determined by the producer alone, however; it is determined on the market by supply and demand. A commonly made mistake is to call these prices thus determined equilibrium prices. Equilibrium prices, however, only exist when there is a situation of perfect market conditions, a situation that rarely exists in reality.

In a model, perfect competition is represented through supply and demand curves, which illustrate how a market reaches an equilibrium where supply for every product equals demand. The corresponding price is the equilibrium price (Fig. 5.1).

In reality market prices are **not** equilibrium prices since:

1. There is no perfect competition because of factors such as the existence of monopsonies (one single buyer) and oligopsonies (few buyers). These factors have a great impact on the market, resulting in no perfect competition.
2. Countries often impose import and/or export restrictions, or subsidize certain products (think of the large agricultural subsidies in the US and the EU).
3. Then there is also political interference by governments and from pressure groups on governments.
4. Corruption and bad governance can play a role.

[1] Usually the producer has to pay taxes over the sales as well, but since these are so different from one country to another, in the text is refrained from these

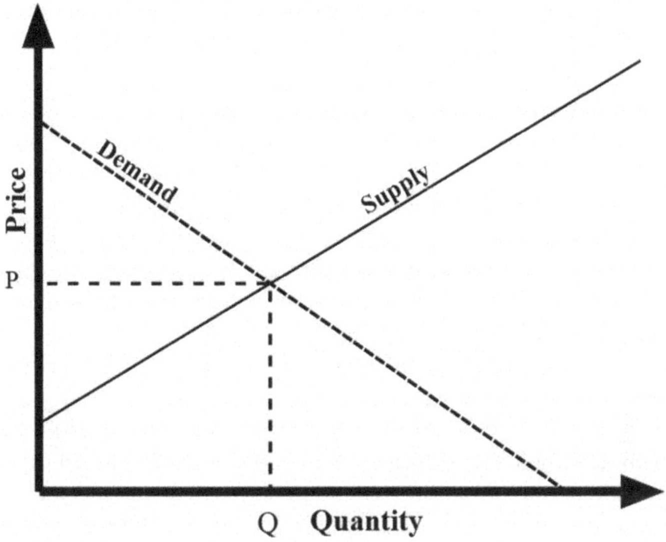

Fig. 5.1 Equilibrium price P at quantity Q

5. There is also the important point that the demand side consists of effective demand only, meaning that only the demand of those people who can afford to buy is taken into consideration. This means that the demand of people with no or few financial resources is not taken into account. Hence it is important to realize that **the demand of the poorest is not taken into account in the equilibrium price.** This is the case for all products, but is especially relevant for food products. This absence is important since food is essential to survive.

For the supply side it is important to take into consideration that supply not only depends on the quantities producers will supply. What is produced depends on the costs of production, the prices of productive services and the level of technical knowledge, as stated by Walras, but also on the needs of the producers themselves, which implies that producers may sell for a price lower than the actual production price in order to gain a living. Of course, they cannot continue infinitely selling at too low a price, but they may save on expenses like schooling for children, hospital visits and so on and thus survive. While with the demand function the fact is that demand can be diminished, or totally withdrawn, when consumers prefer other goods, with the production function this is not always the case. This supply function is in reality often distorted by the fact that there are no other viable options for the producer.

What is needed is a *paradigm change* from the use of prices decided by the market with all its imperfections to an approach founded on ethics. 'Ethical' here is based on Universal Human Rights and implies that any worker receives a decent income for full-time, sustainable work.

In most countries there is some or more protection against market distortions. To protect the consumers there are laws to protect their rights. For producers, however, there are few laws to protect them from being exploited, and only in some countries.

This could be changed by taking not only into account imperfections (who dominates the market) on the supply side such as monopolies and oligopolies, but by also looking at imperfections that prohibit the producer from getting a decent price for his product (monopsonies, oligopsonies). Markets only function well when all participants receive a decent share. When this is not the case for producers, they will take every opportunity to change to other methods of acquiring income. This may lead to a change to other occupations. This is positive as long as alternatives are available. Where these alternatives are not available, workers who do not receive a decent pay for their work are blocked. This partly explains the exodus from rural areas by youth to cities and rich countries or regions, looking for income and a better life.

While a decent remuneration is something workers have a right to already, the payment of decent wages is even more important when the workers have no alternative.

Rules should be set for the minimum income, comparable with those that already exist in the form of legal minimum wages. Legal minimum wages are not always based on a solid calculation of the workers needs, however, as all kinds of political and business-related interests also play a role. Minimum wages and prices should be based on a good calculation of the living wage and the living income. These minimum prices and wages are not only the responsibility of governments, but of companies as well.

Then all producers remain free as to what to produce, how and where, but the rules are changed in such a way that all participants in the chain, from producer to consumer, get a fair share.

CHAPTER 6

Living Wage, Living Income and Fair Price Further Explained

Abstract Here, we will take a closer look at the practical implications of three important concepts:

For Wage earners: Living Wage
For Farmers: Living Income
For All: Fair Producer Prices

In the preceding chapters, definitions are given of Living Wages and Living Income. In order to calculate a Living Income for a farmer, we take the Living Wage multiplied by the number of adult household workers. To this, an additional percentage is added to enable for investments to improve future yields.

A **'Fair' Price** is the minimum price the producer should receive in order to cover all production costs (fixed and variable costs) and be able to pay Fair Wages to all his/her workers on this product and himself/herself. It should also allow the producer to make necessary investments. In the case of agriculture, it should provide at least a 'Living Income' for the farmer.

Keywords Living Wage • Living Income • Fair producer prices • Paradigm change

R. Bronkhorst, *The Economics of Human Rights*,
https://doi.org/10.1007/978-3-030-59166-3_6

We will now take a closer look at the practical implications of three important concepts:

For Wage earners: Living Wage
For Farmers: Living Income
For All: Fair Producer Prices

As already mentioned in Chap. 3, an important definition of **Living Wage** has been formulated by the Global Living Wage Coalition:

> Remuneration received for a standard work week by a worker in a particular place sufficient to afford a decent standard of living for the worker and her or his family. Elements of a decent standard of living include food, water, housing, education, health care, transport, clothing, and other essential needs, including provision for unexpected events. (Global Living Wage Coalition)

In practical terms this means that in order to calculate the living wage, the cost of living must be known, as well as family size and the number of (potential) workers in the family. Costs of living include food, housing, other essential needs and a small margin for unforeseen events. Costs are calculated by estimating the cost of a basic but decent lifestyle for a worker and his/her family (Anker and Anker). It is important to note that these costs are very different from one country to another, because costs of a decent diet can be different from one country to another depending on the kind of food available. Even within countries, especially between rural and urban areas, differences can be great. Housing norms can be very different depending on climatic conditions. Local norms and habits should be represented in the calculations.

In Chap. 3 the following definition of Living Income was given: "A **Living Income** is the net income of a household earned/generated under conditions of decent work, sufficient to enable all members of the (average) household to afford a decent standard of living." I propose to add a percentage for additional investments and use this extended definition in this book.

In order to calculate a Living Income for a farmer we take the Living Wage multiplied by the number of adult household workers. An additional percentage is added to allow for investments to improve future yields.

A **'Fair' Price** is the minimum price the producer should receive in order to cover all production costs (fixed and variable costs) and be able to pay Fair Wages to all his/her workers on this product and him/herself. It should also allow the producer to make necessary investments. In the case of agriculture it should provide at least a 'Living Income' for the farmer (see Part II on Agriculture).

A 'Fair' price must include at least the payment of 'Fair Wages': wages sufficient to enable the worker to have a decent life for himself and for his family. This includes education, health care and shelter, on the condition that a complete working week is spent on this production and the product is one that is useful. A way to determine the usefulness of the product is by the demand for the article.[1] Along with coverage of production costs, a reasonable profit must be part of the fair price. A reasonable profit is a profit that permits the firm to continue its operations and make the necessary investments to be able to continue in the future as well. Think, for instance, of investments needed to prepare for climate change. How much this reasonable profit should be can be decided on a case-by-case basis.

The income of the producer, whether this is a company or an individual who hires a working force, determines the wages that can be paid to the workers. When the income of the producer is too low, living wages cannot be paid.

In order to proceed with a Fair Price calculation, attention should be paid to the following:

The price the producer gets for his/her products should be at least such that:

(a) the price is sufficient to pay all costs, both fixed and variable;
(b) this price is sufficient to guarantee continuity of the enterprise;
(c) all labour involved get paid at least a 'Fair Wage' as well as the legal minimum wage;
(d) the producer himself has an income that equals at least both the 'Fair Wage' as well as the legal minimum wage;
(e) this price is sufficient to make necessary additional investments.

[1] Usefulness cannot be measured by demand alone. There are many products that are in high demand (such as certain drugs) but that are harmful both to the user as well as to the general health system.

There is a difference in defining fair prices between fair producer prices and fair consumer prices. A fair price to the producer essentially means that he/she is not paid too little, while a fair price to the consumer means that he/she is not paying too much for a decent product.

A fair price to the consumer is based on the consumer's preference to pay, whereby the willingness to pay can be restrained by lack of monetary means. It implies the absence of excess profits in the chain, due to monopolies, oligopolies and other factors. A fair price to the consumer does not imply that the lowest possible amount is paid, but that not unduly much or little is paid. This means that a fair price to the consumer implies a fair price to the producer.

A fair price to the producer is based on a needs-assessment of the producer, based on the average size of the households in the area, in agriculture average production per hectare, and on the assumption that all labour is used for this work.

In order to give producers and workers the possibility of earning at least a Fair Wage, and farmers of earning a Living Income, the conclusion will again be that a ***paradigm change*** is needed in our thinking about prices.

In Part II about Agriculture we will see that in order to calculate a fair price for agricultural products the analysis has to be even further refined, especially as generally the farmer grows several crops, and there are periods when all the time available is used for labour and there are slack times where no work on the land can be done.

CHAPTER 7

Poverty Lines: How to Use Them for Poverty Alleviation

Abstract A number of poverty lines exist. The most common are the poverty lines calculated by the World Bank (WB). The International Poverty Line has a value of US$1.90 PPP.

Another often used poverty line is the national poverty line. This line is calculated by the government of the country itself; so it is not affected by the problems involved in PPPs. A danger that exists here is political involvement.

An example is given of the calculation of Living wages in India, based on the national poverty line. The 1998 ETI Living Wage Summit formula is used to calculate living wages based on the poverty line. Calculated living wages in this case are considerably lower than when using the Anker method.

Keywords PPP • Living Wage • India • Poverty Line

Good calculated poverty lines can in some cases replace the calculation of living wages, especially where it is difficult to obtain the necessary data.

A number of poverty lines exist. The most common are the poverty lines calculated by the World Bank (WB). The International Poverty Line has a value of US$1.90 PPP, the Lower Middle Income Class Poverty Line has a value of US$3.20 PPP and the Upper Middle Income Class Poverty

R. Bronkhorst, *The Economics of Human Rights*,
https://doi.org/10.1007/978-3-030-59166-3_7

Line has a value of US$5.50 PPP.[1] By use of the Purchasing Power Parity (PPP) amounts in US$ can be converted into local currency. PPPs are a way to compare the purchasing power of two countries and are based on representative baskets of goods. However, PPPs[2] do not take into account the specific conditions of specific parts of the population, such as the poorest. PPP does not fit their diets; it compares on the basis of middle-class incomes. WB publishes yearly PPPs, which can be found at https://data.worldbank.org/indicator/PA.NUS.PRVT.PP. Since these data are never actual data (at least one year old), that figure when applied has to be adjusted to the inflation rates of both the country of research and the US.

Asia Floor Wage Alliance (AFWA) calculates yearly PPP$ built on the consumption of goods and services by people, which allows the comparison of the standard of living between countries, regardless of the national currency. The Asia Floor Wage is based on a living wage formula for Asia, calculated by an alliance of Asian trade unions and labour. The PPPs are different in each country's national currency, but with a unit of USD-PPP one has the power to buy the same set of goods and services in all countries.[3] For 2017 the Asia Floor Wage is calculated to be PPP$ 1181. Thus here they work with a very large generalization.

Another often used poverty line is the national poverty line. This line is calculated by the government of the country itself and thus it is not affected by the problems involved in PPPs. A danger that exists here is political involvement; it may be in the interest of the government to have a high or a low poverty line. A lower poverty line might be desired for the inherent possibilities of receiving extra external financial support. A higher poverty line might be interesting if a country prefers to look better in international comparisons. Here the same argument applies as in the case of the minimum wage: there may be several political reasons why the results of the calculation of the poverty line and the minimum wage are higher or lower. Further, and this is the problem with any definition, be it poverty line, living wage or living income, where do you draw the line between acceptable and non-acceptable? Take housing: Is a slum a decent place to live in and, if not, what amenities does housing need to qualify?

[1] Source: http://povertydata.worldbank.org/poverty/home/.

[2] The advantage of this method is that it allows for a rapid comparison of income worldwide. The disadvantage is that PPP becomes available only years later and that it does not take into account regional and country-specific differences (e.g. in food habits).

[3] For the calculation see https://asia.floorwage.org/calculating-a-living-wage.

There are international (UN-Habitat) and national standards that can be used, but national standards may differ greatly from country to country.

Case Study of India

In a paper about fair prices and wages for Indian artisans in 2004, the official poverty line per state was taken as the basis to calculate living wages (Bronkhorst 2004).[4,5] In this case a narrow definition of living wage is used, a wage that is just above the poverty line instead of a decent wage as defined by the Ankers. Therefore these Living Wages could be called 'poverty line wages' as well, as suggested by Krain and Steffens.

Table 7.1 shows the poverty lines for Rajasthan, Delhi and Pondicherry. The poverty line per household is obtained by multiplying the poverty line by average household size (Table 7.2).

Table 7.1 State-wise poverty lines for the year 1999–2000 in Rs per capita per month

State/Union territory	*Rural poverty line*	*Urban poverty line*
Rajasthan	344.03	465.92
Delhi	362.68	505.45
Pondicherry	307.64	475.60

Source: Planning Commission, Government of India

[4] The poverty line per capita in India as defined by the Planning Commission is based on the number of calories needed daily per person. This quantity was defined in 1968 by a Nutrition Expert Group and has been fixed at 2400 calories per capita in rural areas and 2100 calories per capita in urban areas. The difference in quantities of food needed in rural and in urban areas is due to the fact that living conditions in rural areas are more demanding. For instance, people have to walk great distances to access water.

The quantification of the number of calories needed was after research translated into monetary units to answer the question: How much money is spent on average to achieve the necessary quantity of calories? Data for this came from an expenditure survey of the group involved. From this survey it appeared that, based on the actual consumer behaviour, in 1973–1974 on average Rs 49.09 per month was associated with a daily intake of 2400 calories in rural areas, and Rs 56.64 per month with a daily intake of 2100 calories per capita in urban areas.

Thus the poverty line defined in this way is partly normative and partly behavioural. It indicates the monetary value needed to achieve the specific quantity of calories required, taking into account the need for other, non-food-related, expenses.

[5] The full article is included as Annex B.

Table 7.2 Income needed per household based on poverty line in Rs per month by State/Union Territory

State/Union territory	*Rural*	*Urban*
Rajasthan	1927	2330
Delhi	1596	2224
Pondicherry	1292	1902

Table 7.3 Amount of the Living Wage per month in Rs by state/Union Territory in case of one income earner per household

	Amount living wage (Rs)	
State/Union territory	*Rural*	*Urban*
Rajasthan	2141	2588
Delhi	1773	2471
Pondicherry	1436	2114

Table 7.3 shows living wages based upon the poverty line for rural and urban areas based on calculations of one income earner per household (Table 7.3). This is done through application of *The 1998 ETI Living Wage Summit formula* (Steele)

$$\frac{\text{Average household size} \times \begin{pmatrix}\text{cost of basic}\\ \text{needs per person}\end{pmatrix}}{\begin{matrix}\text{Average number of adult}\\ \text{earners per household}\end{matrix}} + \text{savings}\ (\text{set at } 10\% \text{of income})$$

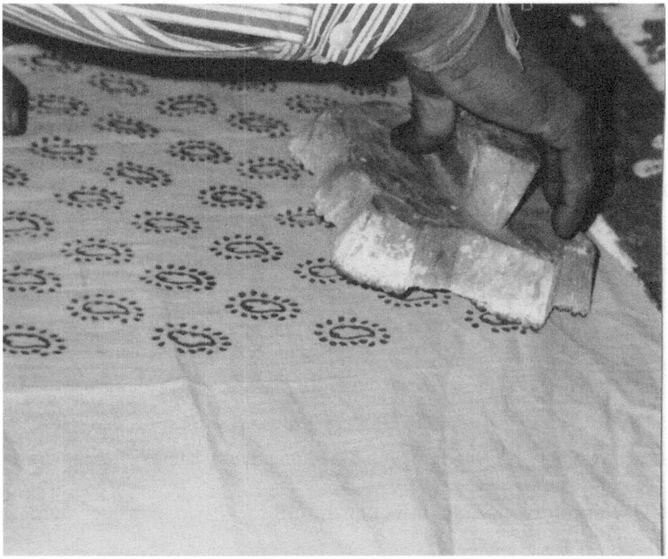

'Blockprinting in India'. (Photo by author)

The amount of Living Wage based on one or one and a half income earner(s) is equivalent, namely the amount of the Living Wage with one income earner. The amount that has to be earned per household remains the same, the only difference being that it is earned by one or one and a half person/people. Hence in the following this amount of one person is used for the Living Wage.

The calculation from poverty line to Living Wage was made on the basis of poverty lines, average household sizes and labour force participation rates, all state-wise (see Annex B for a detailed calculation).

For urban areas this results in Fig. 7.1.

And for rural areas in Fig. 7.2.

It is clear that in both cases (urban and rural) payment of workers on the level of the poverty line (which represents the income needs of an individual) is not sufficient to keep a household running, and hence payment at the level of a Living Wage is necessary. Only when this condition is met can a family live on an income slightly higher than the absolute minimum. Whether this is sufficient is a political question to be answered. Note, however, that the amount of the Living Wage thus calculated is considerably lower than when calculated according to the Anker method.

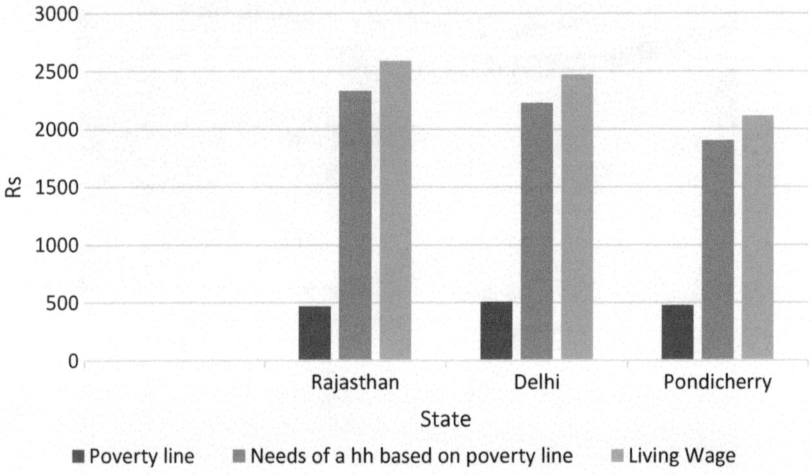

Fig. 7.1 Minimum amounts in Rs per month for urban areas per state

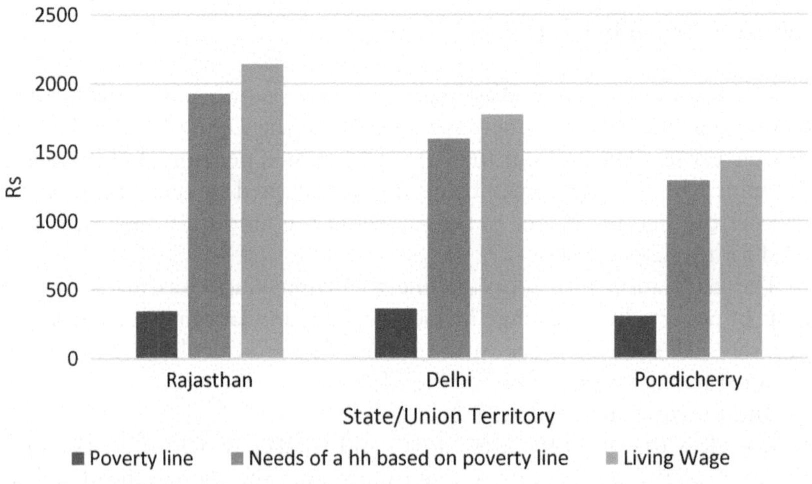

Fig. 7.2 Minimum amounts in Rs per month for rural areas per state

Also note that this calculation was made on the data that existed at the time. Since then the organization WageIndicator Foundation has published many living wages around the world. This is very useful, although these calculations reflect often nationwide data or concern one region, and data are not always dealing with the exact target group for which you want information (www.wageIndicator.org).

Additionally, the Global Living Wage Coalition has calculated living wages in different countries for several regions and target groups (https://www.globallivingwage.org/).

CHAPTER 8

How a Different Way of Calculating in the Production Chain Can Lead to a more Equal Share for All Stakeholders

Abstract Only a very small part of the value added in the chain goes to the worker. A simple example shows how wages at the start of the chain can be increased without leading to great price increases for the consumers at the end of the chain, by a change in calculation methodology. When price increases are measured in money instead of in percentages, every part of the chain other than the workers will continue to have the same profit as before, while the workers will gain more. The effects of doubling of wages on consumer price are shown.

Keywords Calculation example • Wages • Chain • Effects price increases

A 2016 report by the International World Union Confederation titled 'Scandal: Inside the global supply chains of 50 top companies' shows the breakdown of costs of a shirt. It appears that of the total costs of the shirt of € 29, only a very small part (€ 0.18) goes to the worker.

That small farmers often are the worst off in the supply chain is demonstrated in the 2014 study 'Who's got the Power,' among others (Basic) (see also Part II, pp. 76–77).

A simple example shows how wages at the start of the chain can be increased without leading to great price increases for the consumers at the end of the chain, by a change in calculation methodology. When price

R. Bronkhorst, *The Economics of Human Rights*,
https://doi.org/10.1007/978-3-030-59166-3_8

increases are measured in money instead of in percentages every part of the chain other than the workers will continue to have the same profit as before, while the workers will gain more.

Calculation Example

Below is a simple model showing the differences in consumer price when calculations are made with fixed amounts instead of percentages. Note that this model is only a model to show how different methods of calculation have different results (Table 8.1).

Table 8.1 Effects of doubling of wages on consumer price

	Initial wages of €20	*Doubling of wages, other cost increases in %*		*Doubling of wages, other cost increases in fixed amounts*	
Description	€	%	€	%	€
Labour	20		40		40
Material	20		20		20
Rent	5		5		5
Other costs	5		5		5
Total production costs	50		70		70
Profit	5	10%	7	10%	5
Subtotal	55		77		75
Transport	8	15%	12	15%	8
Subtotal	63		89		83
Shipping and handling	13	20%	18	20%	13
Subtotal	76		106		96
Transport and handling costs	4	5%	5	5%	4
Country of destination					
Storage	4	5%	5	5%	4
Subtotal	83		117		103
Profit importer	17	20%	23	20%	17
Subtotal	100		140		120
Costs and profit retailer	30	30%	42	30%	30
Subtotal	130		182		150
Taxes 10%	13	10%	18	10%	15
Consumer price	143		201		165

The practice is that the rise in costs is often calculated by percentages. Each new intermediary adds a certain percentage on the cost price thus far, for example 15, 20 or 30%.

Here this leads from a total of initial production costs of € 50, of which € 20 is labour costs, to a consumer price of € 143.

A doubling of wages from € 20 to € 40 would lead to production costs of € 70, and ultimately to a consumer price of € 201, which is indeed quite a difference from € 143. A rise in the consumer price of €58 will usually lead to fewer buyers, as long as the product is not essential.

If the new consumer price is calculated by taking the same margins for intermediaries as they had been calculated previously in money terms instead of percentages, the effects of the wage increase will be more limited.

In the example the profit of the importer is an amount of € 17, or 20%. If the wages of the workers are doubled from € 20 to € 40, the profit of the importer will rise from € 17 to € 23.

This rise in profit takes place without any more work or costs for him.

If, however, he would be satisfied with the same profit as before, namely € 17, and all others in the chain will do the same, the result will be a consumer price of € 165 instead of € 201. This means that the direct effects of the wage increase are limited to the amount of the wage increase (€ 20) plus more taxes (€ 18 instead of € 13 because these are always expressed as a certain percentage). The consumer will have to pay more (€ 165 instead of € 143), but much less than in the case where percentages are used (€ 165 instead of € 201).

This simple example clearly shows that attention should be paid not only to the workers, but also to all other actors in the chain such as importers and retailers, and to the way calculations are made.

We will now proceed to the question of how Fair Wages can be calculated.

CHAPTER 9

How to Calculate Fair Wages

Abstract On the basis of the calculation of Living Wages, the amounts of Fair Wages can be decided upon in consultation with representatives of the workers themselves.

The calculated amounts for Living Wages as well as the legal minimum wages are the absolute minimum below which Fair Wages cannot fall.

Keywords Data to be collected • Living Wage • Fair Wage

A number of types of data have to be collected.

- The average family size must be known: adults, children below 16, children 16–18 years of age and elderly above the age of 60;
- The total expenses of the family during the year, on both food and non-food products needed for a 'basic but decent living standard';
- To this some 10% must be added for additional and often unforeseen expenses (the exact percentage depends on local circumstances);
- Average number of adult earners per family must be known;
- Number of working days per year = calendar days - (Sundays or any other weekly holiday, such as Friday or Saturday) - festivals - social obligations - calamities - sick days.

R. Bronkhorst, *The Economics of Human Rights*,
https://doi.org/10.1007/978-3-030-59166-3_9

With these data, the Living Wage per adult earning family member per working day can be calculated.

LW per person (pp) per year = Family income needed divided by number of adult income earners

LW pp per day = LW per year divided by number of working days

On the basis of those calculations, the amounts of Fair Wages can be decided upon, in consultation with representatives of the workers themselves, as advised by Vaughan-Whitehead, with these amounts for Living Wages as well as the legal minimum wages as the absolute minimum below which Fair Wages cannot fall.

As mentioned in Chap. 4, it is important to realize that for the producer to be able to pay Fair Wages, the Living Wage must be known, there must be an effective demand for the product, and the consumer must have the financial resources needed to purchase the product.

Let's now have a further look at the possible effects the payment of Fair Wages and Fair Prices will have on the socio-economic development of the region where this is implemented. This is in order to have a clear view of what the social and economic effects can be when this application of Human Rights is put into practice.

CHAPTER 10

Effects of Payment of Fair Wages and Prices on Socio-economic Development

Abstract Payment of living wages and fair prices can have effects on both macro and micro levels. The payment of 'fair prices' to producers and fair wages to workers leads to an effect on the whole society. Fair Prices are based on the assumption that Fair Wages are paid to all workers involved, and Living Incomes to farmers.

Both economic and social effects are discussed. Economic effects include the effects of higher wages and fair prices on purchasing power, turnover, profits, employment, government budget and migration. Social effects not only include positive effects on the health of the workers and their families, possibilities for schooling for the children and in general, 'welfare' effects, but also negative effects such as the widening of the gap in income between workers employed by different companies. Also, destruction of traditional ways of living and society that can lead to social unrest must be mentioned.

Keywords Economic • Social • Effects • Purchasing power • Turnover • Profits • Employment • Government budget • Migration • South Africa

The amount of fair wages to be paid must be taken into account in the calculation of the sales price of the firm. This implies that the sales price should be such that all production costs and at least 'Fair Wages' for the

R. Bronkhorst, *The Economics of Human Rights*,
https://doi.org/10.1007/978-3-030-59166-3_10

producer and all workers are included. Production costs also include transport and distribution costs, depreciation and investment costs.

An often-used argument against the payment of fair or living wages is that it is economically not feasible. Let us therefore take a closer look at the possible effects of payment of these wages.

When we look at the population as producers and consumers it is clear that their interests do not always match. Part of the population is producer, and another part is consumer. But a great part of the population is both producer and consumer. A price increase of a certain good may lead to more income for the producer and, because of that price increase, a lower income to be spent by the consumer. Thus a decent income for the food producer may be ethically necessary, but will this not lead to such a decline in the spendable income of the consumer that the result is worse than the cure?

Payment of living wages and fair prices can have effects on both a macro and micro level. The payment of 'fair prices' to producers and fair wages to workers leads to an effect on the whole society. Fair Prices are based on the assumption that Fair Wages are paid to all workers involved, and Living Incomes to farmers.

Suppose that in a specific region wages are increased to a level above the common paid wages and achieve the level of a 'Living Wage.'

We can distinguish between economic and social effects. Economic effects include the effects of higher wages and fair prices on purchasing power, turnover, profits, employment, government budget and migration. Social effects not only include positive effects on the health of the workers and their families, possibilities for schooling for the children and in general 'welfare' effects, but also negative effects such as the widening of the gap in income between workers employed by different companies. We must also mention destruction of traditional ways of living and society, which can lead to social unrest.

Economic Effects

Purchasing Power

A rise in wages leads to more purchasing power for the workers involved, which has an impact on the economy. Because of the rise in income, effective demand for goods gets a boost. What is important for the economy is to know what demand for which goods rises. Take a family that before the rise in wages did not have enough to eat. It is likely that they will use a great part of the additional income to purchase more, or better, food.[1] Other products will follow in order of preference. Because of a multiplier effect, trade in these specific products rises and thus shopkeepers have a larger turnover and local producers can produce more, as long as domestic products are consumed. This may also have a negative effect though: If shopkeepers adjust the prices to the new purchasing power, people who are already poor and who do not work in the respective sector will be worse off, not only in relative but also in absolute terms.

If, however, most of the additional wages are used to purchase foreign goods, the local economy profits much less because only importers and retailers profit, and not local industry. In that case a great part of the wages leaks away. Hence the import quote is very important. Since the benefits of increased wages are destined for those workers who have an income below or around the poverty line, however, this leakage will probably not be too large a part of the accrued income.

For local, village and rural shops an increased consumption level by a number of families can make a difference. How much difference depends on the level at which living wages have been applied. The more companies pay a fair wage to their workers, the more the local economy profits. When production by these companies is for export mainly, the amount of wages paid comes from abroad. If this is spent on local goods, the local economy profits. When spent on imported goods, however, the local economy benefits to a lesser degree.

Turnover

What will be the effects on turnover, profits and employment? All variables are linked. For a firm a diminishing turnover leads to lower production, fewer profits and lower employment, while a higher turnover, when techniques remain the same, leads to more production, more profits and more employment. So we must also pose the question of what the effects of higher wages on turnover will be. Higher wages in one firm will normally not lead to a higher turnover of that same firm.

At first glance an effect of higher wages and fair prices will be that turnover will diminish because consumer prices will rise because of higher

[1] Banerjee and Duflo give examples why more income may be used for items to make life more pleasant instead of on food.

wages paid. If demand is relatively inelastic,[2] however, firms may be able to increase their prices and maintain their output.

There are a number of arguments that indicate why higher wages will not always result in a lower turnover:

1. In case there is a situation of inelastic demand, consumers will continue to purchase even in spite of a price rise.
2. Consumer prices for a number of products in Europe and other wealthy countries can be increased when production is destined for a niche in the market. People are willing to pay more for an exclusive product. How much more they are willing to pay depends on the elasticity of their demand.
3. A rise in wages does not in all cases necessarily lead to much higher prices for the consumers. This requires a different method of calculating the consumer price, namely by not working with percentages in the chain but with fixed prices. In Chap. 8, Table 8.1 a very simplified model is given showing the differences in consumer prices when calculations are done with fixed amounts instead of percentages.
4. Costs, and thus prices, can be lowered by more cooperation in the fields of transport, both national and international, and storage. This may take the form of, for instance, common warehouses, common use of a container to ship goods and the mutual use of the same exporter.

These arguments show that higher wages can, but do not automatically have to, result in a lower turnover. In case of a drop in turnover, the question is whether this can be made up for by applying the recommendations for improved cooperation and calculation methods in the chain. It is quite possible however, that higher wages lead to a drop in demand. In that case the producer will be left with unsold products with all the resulting consequences.

Unfortunately, it is not possible to formulate general rules; for each situation and each product the situation can be different.

The OECD writes in its 2016 publication "Scaling Up Living Wages in Global Supply Chains" under point 5 "It pays to pay a living wage" of their

[2] An inelastic price means that if the price is increased the quantity demanded will not fall as much proportionally and therefore the total expenditure on the good will increase.

Working Paper "Responsible Business Conduct and Responsible Supply Chains": "Apart from ethical considerations, there are many reasons why it makes business sense to strive for payment of living wage throughout the value chain. Paying relatively low wages may lead to costs for businesses such as lower product quality, lower worker productivity and few investments in innovation due to high labor-turnover. Below living wages also increase the risk of labor unrest which can lead to the disruptions of operations and reputational damage to companies, particularly in this age of mass communication. Lastly the rise in ethical consumerism means that companies can access an important market share and stand to profit by behaving responsibly". (Nieuwenkamp and Hennis)

Profits

If demand is relatively inelastic, firms may be able to increase prices when wages are increased and yet maintain their output.

If turnover in case of a wage increase is not diminished and consumer prices remain at the same level as before, what happens to profits as wages are higher now than before? If demand remains stable, and techniques used in the production phase and prices of intermediate goods remain the same, profits will fall, unless the benefits generated by more cooperation in the chain, a different method of calculation in the chain, and better adjustment to changing demand compensate for this. What is important in this respect is to what extent the producer is able to invest in better techniques. Here the possibilities of credit and support by intermediate buyers are important, as is analysis of the whole chain. Are there any excess profits in the chain?

Example

When we look at the example of bananas (Part II), it appears that traders take 40% of the value share and the farmers and workers 11.5% only. This gives at least the impression that both wages and profits could be raised if traders were to take a lower share. A thorough examination of the chain must make clear whether this is feasible.

When paying higher wages to their labourers, employers will be able to choose the best workers, leaving their competitors with the less able and educated. "Essentially, paying higher wages can be perceived as a management strategy to achieve increased worker productivity and greater total efficiency" (Jacques, 103).

Thus profits may suffer from higher wages, but there are other ways to make up for this and sometimes profits can even rise.

Employment

The arguments above seem to indicate that the payment of a fair price does not necessarily lead to a dramatic rise in consumer prices and therefore to a great loss in turnover. What it does lead to is a change in production costs with a higher cost for labour.

So even if the effects of a change in turnover on employment are minimal, changes because of higher remuneration of labour may lead to pressure on the number of workers.

It is possible that a producer invests in labour-saving techniques because wages become too high. In that case often higher-skilled labourers will be needed who usually have to be better paid as well. These investments, if well managed, may lead to a better position for the higher-skilled workers in the market, with the side effect of an increase in demand for higher-skilled labour at the cost of unskilled labour.

A negative effect of higher wages can be that the trend of production work being moved from rich countries to poor countries is reversed. Production work that is now done in countries with low wages could be moved to other low-wage countries, where wages are even lower. This is now already the case with industries that move their production locations from China to other low-wage countries.

Where large numbers of unskilled labour are needed, payment of higher wages may lead to greater demand for jobs with companies that pay a higher wage, and a subsequent decline in offers of unskilled labour with companies that pay low wages. Seasonal labour will more easily move from a place where low wages are paid to another place where wages are higher.

Thus where there are large groups of seasonal labourers who move from one place and one country to another, an effect will be that they will tend to move to places with the highest wages. Employers who pay higher wages will thus be able to choose the best labourers for the job, while the lower-paying employers are left with those who do not qualify for the best remunerated jobs.

Therefore the result of higher wages on employment, even when the chain is better organized, is different from place to place and will not be the same everywhere.

Box 10.1 Imposition of a minimum wage in South Africa

In South Africa, in the case of agriculture, the imposition of a minimum wage had a swift and large negative impact on employment. Employment fell in the year after the imposition of the minimum wage in 2003 by close to 150,000 workers, representing a 17% decline. In turn, farm owners did not reduce hours worked in a bid to control higher wage costs, as hours worked after the minimum wage was introduced did not change significantly. Farmworkers gained, however, as estimates show that farmworker wages in the post-law period increased on average by 17.6%. Finally, worker protection improved, as the share of workers with a written employment contract rose sharply from 34% in the pre-law period to reach 57% by the end of 2007.

Evidence for the retail, domestic worker and private security sectors suggests that the probability of attaining employment in these sectors was significantly higher in the period after the introduction of minimum wages. These are the sectors where the employment numbers continued to rise after minimum wage laws were enacted. This suggests that employers may have started to reduce the usual work hours of employees in order to afford higher hourly wages. However, when investigating the effect of the laws on real monthly income, the retail, domestic work and security sectors showed an increase in real hourly wages that was sufficient to outweigh any reductions in hours worked–workers ended up being better off in the aggregate.

> "*Ultimately though, this study illustrates the care that needs to be taken when attempting to pre-judge the potential economic consequences arising from the imposition of a minimum wage. Factors as wide-ranging as the level at which the minimum wage is set, the economic conditions prevalent within the sector, the wage elasticity and so on – all serve to influence the impact of an instrument which has become a key active labour market policy intervention in the developing world*". (Bhorat World Bank Blog)

Box 10.2 Another view on effects of minimum wage
Another view on the issue is given by Ximena Del Carpio and Ha Minh Nguyen. They write that several studies find that increases in minimum wages without commensurate increases in labour productivity could lead to job losses in the formal sector. The main reason provided for this argument is that poor workers—the people expected to benefit from the policy—are more likely to be pushed out of formal employment because they often have limited skills and low productivity, and thus tend to be among the first to be laid off when minimum wages increase. (Del Carpio and Nguyen World Bank Blog)

Effects on Government Budget

All interventions that imply additional government expenses have negative effects on government expenses. Examples of these are subsidies on food, security and intervention stocks, subsidies on inputs and support to projects. They all have negative effects on the government budget.

Lower exports mean lower revenues from export taxes. Lower imports may imply lower import taxes received and are as such a drain on the country's financial resources. Higher import tariffs, on the other hand, lead to higher government revenues.

In countries where an efficient tax system exists, more income by the workers may lead to more government revenues through income tax and VAT. Especially when the wages are paid by foreign investors, the effect on government revenues is positive.

Migration

Here we must distinguish between seasonal and permanent migration. Seasonal migration happens everywhere labour moves from one place to another to find employment. A good example of this is seasonal labour in agriculture: labour follows agricultural seasons.

Other important reasons for migration can be war and natural disasters, such as earthquakes, floods and draughts.

Permanent migration is not always intended: people migrate because of what is considered a temporary situation, which develops over time into a permanent situation. Permanent migration is an important topic in political debates in Western countries at the moment. There are many efforts to bring an end to 'unwanted' migration, such as building walls at the borders (the US, Hungary) and making deals with countries of transit (the EU with Turkey) and with countries of origin (the EU with African countries). The causes of these migrations may be climate change, civil unrest, natural disasters or lack of income. Wesselbaum and Aburn state that climate change is a more important driver than income and political freedom at origin together (Wesselbaum and Aburn), while Kirwin and Anderson conclude that "Promoting good governance rather than economic development could be more effective in providing West Africans with the hope that they can live a fulfilling life in their country of origin" (Kirwin and Anderson, 19).

When individuals and enterprises have sufficient income, they can prepare themselves for outside shocks and catastrophes/disasters. Sufficient income is essential to enable people to take appropriate measures rather than having to escape.

Seasonal migration is different from permanent migration. Payment of fair wages makes it more attractive for seasonal labourers to move to those areas where their pay is most attractive. This may lead to large migration flows, such as in the case of India where workers move from, among other states, Bihar to other Indian states to work in factories, in mining and so on, and in Southern Africa where large numbers of labourers move from one country to another to work.

Social Effects

Along with economic effects there may be social effects as well:

1. A rise in income is always welcomed by the worker and his family. They can then afford for themselves and their family better and healthier food, better treatment in case of illness and schooling for their children—in short, both more welfare and greater well-being. To this must be added that healthier food, especially during infancy, and better medical care lead to an increase in productivity and thus have an economic effect as well. This also enables marginalized and have deprived people to set their own priorities. It can provide a boost for a decent life and food security for both farmer and labourer and their families, and stimulate sustainable agricultural practices.

Above the importance of good governance was underlined. Ensuring a decent income for a country's citizens and that everybody receives a fair share of a growing national income is a characteristic of good governance.

2. The gap between well-paid workers and others grows. In some instances one might say that an island is created of 'fair' paid workers in the middle of a mass of underpaid workers. This may create jealousy from the other workers but might also have a positive effect on other employers and employees because they see that the payment of a fair wage is possible.
3. Payment of fair prices and wages can lead to other, more capital-intensive, methods of production, thereby destroying existing socio-cultural communities and ways of living. This may also lead to more unemployment and growing social unrest. Such a change should be carefully monitored and not be analysed from an economic point of view only.
4. The social effects of migration can be profound. Children grow up without their father and/or mother, and families are often torn apart in the case of temporary migration. With permanent migration come the problems of adapting to a foreign, and sometimes even hostile, environment. This all puts a severe strain on social relations.

CHAPTER 11

Conclusions on Economic and Social Effects

Abstract Here, conclusions regarding the effects of the payment of Fair wages and prices are summarised, while taking into account that it is difficult to draw uniform conclusions, because each situation and each product is different and requires a separate analysis. Yet a number of conclusions can be drawn.

Keywords Conclusions economic and social effects • CRS • Employment • Profits • Purchasing power • Migration

On the basis of this we come to the following conclusions regarding the effects of the payment of Fair wages and prices:

1. Uniform conclusions cannot be drawn because each situation and each product is different and requires a separate analysis.
2. Payment of fair wages will lead to rising purchasing power for the workers involved, resulting in more welfare and higher well-being for the workers whose wages have risen.
3. More purchasing power of the workers will have a positive effect on the local economy.
4. Payment of higher wages may lead to additional costs for the producer.

R. Bronkhorst, *The Economics of Human Rights*,
https://doi.org/10.1007/978-3-030-59166-3_11

5. Employment effects are likely to be negative for unskilled and low-skilled labour, but may be positive for higher-skilled workers. Where usual work hours were reduced to afford higher wages as in the case of South Africa, employment rose.
6. Profits for the producer are likely to diminish because of higher remuneration of the factor labour. This may stimulate investments in labour-saving techniques.
7. It is not possible to predict the outcome of a rise in prices as a consequence of higher wages for consumers' behaviour in Western countries. A percentage of the consumers will leave because of the higher price; other customers will remain because they find better working conditions important. Consumers attach more and more importance to the Corporate Social Responsibility (CSR) of the companies. They may even stop purchasing certain products if no fair wages are paid to the workers.
8. Turnover may diminish, except in the case of inelastic demand, but this can be stopped and sometimes even reversed by more cooperation in the chain and another method of calculating the consumer price.
9. The effects on government revenues are mixed and should be examined in connection with long-term effects.
10. A demonstration effect on other companies and employees will take place.
11. With more income, marginalized and deprived people can set their own priorities.
12. Attention should be given to side effects such as the destruction of socio-cultural communities and ways of living.
13. Migration and exodus of rural areas will be affected as well.

CHAPTER 12

Broader Context

Abstract The common view that everything the market does is right is heavily debated by neo-classical economists as well. Numerous exceptions have been identified where the market does not behave in a fully satisfactory way, like oligopolies, monopolies and so on. Several economists have taken much more distance from the current neo-classical theory and have published serious criticisms of it.

A concept of 'Fair Trade' was developed, in addition to the concepts Living Wage and Living Income. There is the need to change to a more circular economy. The spread of the Corona virus (Covid-19) has led to a tendency to look more critically at production at different locations in the world.

Keywords Living Wage • Living Income • Covid-19 • Fair Trade

The common view that all the market does is right is also heavily debated by neo-classical economists. Numerous exceptions have been identified where the market does not behave in a fully satisfactory way, such as oligopolies and monopolies.

Several economists have moved away from the current neo-classical theory and have published serious criticisms of it. Annex I mentions some

R. Bronkhorst, *The Economics of Human Rights*,
https://doi.org/10.1007/978-3-030-59166-3_12

critics who have taken into account more than only market equilibrium theories and have introduced power relations into their studies.

A concept of 'Fair Trade' was developed in which fair trade relations were made central. This concept falls within the scope of neo-classical theory. With the general acceptance of some protection against complete free trade, a notion of fair trade or a 'level playing field' was developed. "Fair trade policy is usually quasi-protectionist and multifunctional in terms of its goals, creating policies that take into account economics, development issues, sociological concerns, and politics" (Balaam & Dillman). Fair Trade Organizations use their own concept of fair trade with an additional principle that aims at economically disadvantaged producers (WFTO 2014). Although often paying higher prices than market prices, there is no consensus among fair trade organizations on what is a 'fair' price to the producer. The concept of fair trade held the promise of a change in (international) relationships, but was limited to a marginal position, whereby not even fair prices are guaranteed.

For companies, calculated fair prices can provide a guideline on how to pay minimum ethical prices. The OECD Guidelines for Multinational Enterprises, 2011, state that "when multinational enterprises operate in developing countries, where comparable employers may not exist, [they should] provide the best possible wages, benefits and conditions of work, within the framework of government policies. These should be related to the economic position of the enterprise, but should be at least adequate to satisfy the basic needs of the workers and their families" (Nieuwenkamp and Hennis).

The concepts of Living Wage and Living Income have recently attracted a great deal of attention. Several companies and many NGOs make calculations for living wage and income in their region. The Living Income Community of Practice (a partnership between The Sustainable Food Lab, GIZ and the ISEAL Alliance) provides information on methods to measure and report information on current and living incomes, and how to identify and discuss strategies to help actors take actions that can contribute to closing income gaps (https://www.living-income.com/). The Global Living Wage Coalition has calculated living wages in different countries for several regions and target groups (https://www.globallivingwage.org/). Living wages are calculated by WageIndicator as well (www.wageIndicator.org).

Another aspect that is receiving more and more attention nowadays is the need to change to a more circular economy. "In a circular economy the value of products and materials is maintained for as long as possible; waste and resource use are minimised, and resources are kept within the economy when a product has reached the end of its life, to be used again and again to create further value" (European Commission 2019). Organizations such as True Price (https://trueprice.org/) seek to determine the price at which a product is fully sustainable, meaning no damage done to people or to nature. Part of a true price of products must be a 'fair' price to make sure there is no exploitation of the workers.

For all countries, economic considerations and their importance are not the only base for policies. Other factors play a role as well, especially political considerations. Fear of growing influence by other countries (e.g. the competition between the US and China) is important.

In addition, the spread of disease now plays an important role. For instance, the Coronavirus (Covid-19) has led to a tendency to look more critically at production in different locations in the world.

The same way the Plague (Black Death) in the fourteenth century was transmitted through international trade routes, Covid-19 has spread because of the many international contacts. All regions of the world are interconnected through trade and international tourism. The Covid-19 crisis has shown that producing in different parts of the world can disrupt entire economies. When export from one country becomes impossible, industries in other countries suffer as well.

European countries are now shocked to discover that so many essential medicines come from China and India. This has led to a renewed discussion about the desirability of spreading production worldwide. These discussions may lead to less outsourcing and thus less income for poorer countries. What will be the effects of these developments on the workers? Will they retain their jobs or become part of the desperate masses without work or food? The way the fashion industry has reacted to the Covid-19 pandemic does not bode well for the workers. Thousands of workers have been sacked and sent home without their wages being paid, because the large American and European importers, faced with a stagnation in their sales, have annulled their orders and sometimes even refused to pay for goods already delivered. This way local employers cannot consider raising wages to Fair Wages, but they are glad already when they can keep (part of) their workers.

New international trade routes (new silk roads) are being constructed, but whether this will keep international trade at the same level as it is now is doubtful.

PART II

Agriculture

CHAPTER 13

Introduction

Abstract Agriculture employs one in three people of the world's economically active labour force, or about 1.3 billion people (FAOSTAT 2013, http://www.fao.org/faostat/en/#home). Agriculture is the single largest employer in the world, providing livelihoods for 40% of today's global population. It is the largest source of income and jobs for poor rural households (UN Sustainable Development Goals).

After many years of progress, the absolute number of undernourished people in the world has actually increased in recent years, from 784 million in 2015 to 821 million in 2017. More than 2 billion people lack the micronutrients needed for growth, development and disease prevention (World Bank Food Security).

For the 70 per cent of the world's poor living in rural areas, agriculture is the main source of income and employment (World Bank).

Keywords Rural • Livelihoods • Undernourished • Agriculture

Agriculture employs 1 in 3 people of the world's economically active labour force, or about 1.3 billion people (FAOSTAT 2013). Agriculture is the single largest employer in the world, providing livelihoods for 40 per cent of today's global population. It is the largest source of income and jobs for poor rural households (UN Sustainable Development Goals).

R. Bronkhorst, *The Economics of Human Rights*,
https://doi.org/10.1007/978-3-030-59166-3_13

After many years of progress, the absolute number of undernourished people in the world has actually increased in recent years, from 784 million in 2015 to 821 million in 2017. More than 2 billion people lack the micronutrients needed for growth, development and disease prevention (World Bank Food Security).

For the 70 per cent of the world's poor living in rural areas, agriculture is the main source of income and employment (World Bank).

Almost one billion people are extremely poor (living on less than $1.25 a day) and 78% of the extreme poor are living in rural areas. Another billion are poor (less than $2.00 a day).

More than 90% of the 570 million farms worldwide are managed by an individual or a family, relying predominately on family labour. These farms produce more than 80% of the world's food, in terms of value. Globally, 84% of family farms are smaller than 2 hectares and manage only 12% of all agricultural land. While small farms tend to have higher yields than larger farms, labour productivity is lower and most small family farmers are poor and food-insecure (FAO 2014).

Smallholders manage over 80% of the world's estimated 500 million small farms and provide over 80% of the food consumed in a large part of the developing world, contributing significantly to poverty reduction and food security (IFAD/UNEP).

Investing in smallholders is an important way to increase food security and nutrition for the poorest, as well as food production for local and global markets (UN Sustainable Development Goals).

CHAPTER 14

About Necessity and Possibilities to Pay Fair Prices to Small Farmers

Abstract People go hungry because they lack the monetary resources to purchase the food they need. On the production side it is important to realize that small farmers are only able to produce more when they have the possibility to invest in seeds, equipment, marketing, fertilizer and so on. We can make a mental shift to a situation where the existing theory of supply and demand with all its theoretical assumptions and problems is not at the centre. We can ask ourselves how to use the pricing mechanism to ensure not only a decent life for the consumers, but for the producers as well, thus changing from something nebulous that we cannot influence, to a system where prices are used to achieve a just society in which basic human rights are respected.

Keywords Hunger • Lack of monetary resources • Micro financing • Supply forced by poverty • Household income • Living income

Apart from famines, many people go hungry despite the production of food being sufficient to feed the global population. According to the FAO, food production systems produce approximately 2800 calories per person per day, which is enough to feed the world's population (FAO 2014b).

So why is there hunger when the world's production is enough to feed everybody? There are many possible answers to this, such as natural

R. Bronkhorst, *The Economics of Human Rights*,
https://doi.org/10.1007/978-3-030-59166-3_14

disasters like flooding or draught, situations of war, corruption and lack of political will.

Sen remarked that there are no famines in democratically governed countries, except in case of disasters. This does not, however, exclude the fact that there may be many people going hungry in those countries, only that there are no large-scale famines.

"The causal connection between democracy and the nonoccurrence of famines is not hard to seek. Famines kill millions of people in different countries in the world, but they don't kill the rulers" (Sen 2000). The reason democracy prevents famines, according to Sen, is that this gives the rulers a political incentive to try to prevent famines because they are held accountable.

Yet people go hungry because they lack the monetary resources to purchase the food they need. On the production side it is important to realize that small farmers are only able to produce more when they have the possibility to invest in seeds, equipment, marketing, fertilizer and so on. However, as long they don't even have enough to feed themselves and their family properly, they can't invest. You need to invest to produce more, but to be able to invest you have to produce more. Such is the circle they are locked in.

So why not take a loan in order to invest?

There are a number of reasons why farmers do not make use of micro financing:

- It is not available in the region.
- The formal bank sector is not accessible to them.
- It is available but the costs and interest rates are too high.
- The farmer does not have a security[1] to offer.
- The farmer has a fear of debts.
- There is a lack of a stable environment; a (political) environment is necessary where people feel secure about their belongings and their property rights.

As stated in Part I, market prices are usually determined by supply and demand. In conditions of perfect competition this will result in an

[1] See also Hernando de Soto, who writes that the majority of people in developing countries do not have an official title for their property, which is why they can't use it as security and are thus excluded from the credit system.

equilibrium price. In reality there are many market distortions (power positions of market parties such as monopolies and oligopolies, import and export interests, government policies) that cause many market prices not to reflect equilibrium prices.

In addition, small farmers suffer from many market and institutional problems. This means that they have higher transaction costs and don't get as good a price for their produce as larger farmers do—even though they are just as productive as larger farms per unit area, and often more so (see, e.g., Hazell et al., Reardon et al. and Ploeg, van der).

There are still many poor and hungry people today, in spite of global wealth. This must lead us to the question: What is wrong with the global and national distribution of wealth?

Large parts of the population have too little income because the prices they fetch for their products are not sufficient to live on. Think of artisans, small farmers, (agricultural) labourers and so on.

The common opinion is that a market price is the right price, because it is the result of supply and demand. It is a pity that this belief is so widespread, because the market price is only an equilibrium price when and if all conditions are fulfilled. This means perfect competition without distortions such as monopolies, oligopolies and so on. When we look at markets like those for cocoa, bananas, coffee and tea, we see that a few large companies dominate. Since they all want to make as much profit as possible, none of them are inclined to pay more to the producers than the others do. As for the small farmer, he/she does not have a choice; he must accept the price offered to him. As explained in Part I, his/her supply function is in reality often distorted by the fact that there are no other viable options for the producer. Therefore the supply function often shows not a voluntary supply, but a supply forced by poverty.

The fact that small farmers have a very useful role to play, and are in fact indispensable for the global food situation (see previous chapter), is an additional reason why they should earn enough for a decent living. So why is it that they are often paid so little? Why do people stick to the false notion that the market price is the equilibrium price?

Many countries have laws to protect consumers from paying too much for their products. In contrast to the protection of the consumers, (small) producers are taken less care of. Governments are overall more responsive to the needs of the urban population than those of the rural population. For the small farmer who wants to market his products, not only is the price he is paid important, but there are also many other important factors, such as the availability of markets, roads and other infrastructure, the availability and price of inputs, subsidies and taxes, and so on. Although of a different order, also a reliable government must be mentioned here.

In practice, policy makers and researchers pay more attention to these other factors than to prices. These aspects are easier to handle than market prices. Therefore the price received by the producer for his products is often left out of the analysis. Prices are taken as an objective factor that cannot be changed. However, the fact that we are used to considering market prices as natural does not exclude the possibility to take another look at prices and market equilibrium.

We can make a mental shift to a situation where the existing theory of supply and demand with all its theoretical assumptions and problems is not at the centre. We can ask ourselves how to use the pricing mechanism to ensure not only a decent life for the consumers, but for the producers as well, thus changing from something nebulous that we cannot influence, to a system where prices are used to achieve a just society in which basic human rights are respected.

Let us start with the amount a person should earn to achieve an acceptable income.

To calculate a Living Income at the level of the farm as an enterprise we must look at production costs and the need to pay Living Wages to the workers of the firm and for the farmers' own labour. At farm level, however, not only do wages have to be earned, but also enough surplus money to cover additional investments.

The total of all income earned by the members of a household is the household income.

When we call the total of Living Wages in a household 'the Household Living Wage,' for the Household Living Income the total amount of production costs and household living wages should be increased by another 5–10% at the level of the farm to be able to invest in small equipment (hoes, shovels, etc.) and seeds as well. This additional amount for investments is meant for marginal farmers to be able to cope with new challenges they face, such as climate change.

The total is the Living Income at the level of the household.

In Annex IV equations are given for the more mathematical reader to answer the question of how much money the farm should generate to be able to pay Living Wages if all adult workers work all year, full-time, at the farm. This implies calculations as to what crop should be produced with given production methods on a certain type of land in a certain climate to optimize revenues.

Earlier we mentioned the Living Income definition from a workshop hosted by ISEAL and GIZ: "A living income is the net income of a household earned/generated under conditions of decent work, sufficient to enable all members of the (average) household to afford a decent standard of living." As mentioned previously, in our definition a small percentage should be added for necessary additional investments.

For the agricultural workers we may use the following FAO definitions:

- FAO definition of decent rural employment: Decent rural employment is defined as work that provides a living income and reasonable working conditions. It refers to productive and dignified work that enables people—whether self-employed or wage labourers—to provide for themselves and their families, while also ensuring their safety and health at work and providing them with opportunities to voice their concerns. Decent rural employment opportunities ensure a living wage, security in the workplace, access to social protection and respect for fundamental human rights.
- The FAO defines decent employment as work that provides a living income and reasonable working conditions. Work should be remunerative and dignified. It should enable people—whether through self-employment or wage labour—to provide for themselves and their families. Workers should be able to perform their work under safe and healthy conditions and have a voice in the work place (FAO Rural employment).

CHAPTER 15

Fair Price for Agricultural Products

Abstract Farmers must receive a price for their products that enables them to fulfil their basic needs as well as have a small surplus to invest. Yet small farmers are often the worst off when it comes to distribution of value added. This is shown by some examples.

Keywords Living income • Fair price • Fair wage • Banana • Cocoa • Coffee • Sugarcane

A 'fair' price for the producer can be defined as the price for a product that includes all production costs and at least a 'Living Income' (LI) for the farmer and 'Fair Wages' for all workers involved, plus a small percentage for necessary investments. Since small farmers often hire labour on an individual basis for a short period, for the calculations we will use the notion of Living Wage only instead of Fair Wage.

The Living Income of the farmer includes 'Fair or Living Wages' for all workers involved, both hired labour and family labour, as well as funds for additional investments.

The payment should be based on a complete working week spent on this production, and the product should be one that is useful. Because of the assumption of a full working week spent on this particular crop, it is not necessary to separately calculate the number of hours spent on each crop.

R. Bronkhorst, *The Economics of Human Rights*,
https://doi.org/10.1007/978-3-030-59166-3_15

As shown earlier, the LI concept considers the local context, based on which a decent standard of living is defined.

One of the means necessary for agricultural growth is financial means. Farmers can only invest when their basic needs are satisfied. This means that they must receive a price for their products that enables them to fulfil their basic needs as well as have a small surplus to invest.

It is often the case that farm inputs are subsidized (seeds, fertilizer) because otherwise small farmers cannot afford them. This system is vulnerable to fraud and corruption, as is credit. Should the farmer have enough income from the sale of his products, however, he/she can afford to purchase these essential items, without being dependent on governments, financial institutions, NGOs and so on.

Financial institutions do not have to give loans to farmers but can assist them in saving and using their money in a profitable way. Fortunately, many institutions have already shifted their attention from giving loans to helping the customer to save. Thus financial institutions retain their important role, but in a different way.

Both higher prices and responsible lending can lead to:

- Higher production because of more and better inputs;
- Food security and investment possibilities for producers and their families;
- Multiplier effect: more income for the rural sector.

The advantages of higher prices above taking a loan to invest are that the farmer has more financial reserves, resulting in a greater preparedness for difficult periods such as bad harvests because of climate change, political turmoil or other causes. If a loan is taken, the farmer has a better chance of being able to repay these loans.

When we look at the supply chain it appears that small farmers are often the worst off. This is demonstrated in the study 'Who's got the Power,' among others (BASIC). This study published in November 2014 shows that 33% of the value in the sugar cane sector is kept by the retailers, 21% by refineries, 25% by mills, 3% by traders and only 12% by the 2 million growers and workers.

In the case of coffee, roasters take the largest share, namely 45%, and the 25 million farmers and workers only 11%.

With bananas, the traders take 40% of the value share and the farmers and 500,000 workers 11.5%.

With cocoa the data given by BASIC are that branded manufacturers take 40%, retailers 35% and the 14 million growers and workers receive 5% only (BASIC).

Apart from unforeseen emergencies such as war, earthquakes and tsunamis, food always arrives at those places where there is a monetary demand for it. Lack of access to food is normally not restricted by lack of food, but by lack of income. This explains why there are no large famines in Europe or in the US but only in the areas that happen to be poor. The food needed is available; it is simply not available for those who need it but do not have the financial means to purchase it. This happens both in rich and poor countries. Sometimes there are special stores for the poor (e.g. in India) where they can buy food at a lower price, or even receive it for free.

We will now proceed to an explanation of how fair prices can be calculated.

CHAPTER 16

Steps to Be Taken to Calculate Fair Prices

Abstract This chapter provides a step-by-step approach to calculating Living Wages, Living Income and Fair Prices, whereby the difference is highlighted between a situation of full employment and situations where full employment does not exist.

Keywords Living wages • Living income • Fair price • Not-fully employed price

- First Living Wages must be calculated.[1]
    - This means that the average family size must be known: adults, children and people above the age of 60.
    - The total expenses of the household during the year for a basic but decent life on food, housing and other essential needs must be calculated.
    - To this amount of total expenses 5–10% (depending on region, cultural values, etc.) must be added for additional, and often unforeseen, expenses.

[1] For a detailed description of how to calculate Living Wages according to the Anker methodology, see Anker, Richard and Anker, Martha, Living Wages Around the World, Edward Elgar 2017.

R. Bronkhorst, *The Economics of Human Rights*,
https://doi.org/10.1007/978-3-030-59166-3_16

- Average number of adult earners per household must be known.
- Number of working days per year = calendar days – Sundays – festivals – social obligations – calamities – sick days.

From This the Living Wage Per Adult Earning Family Member Per Working Day Can Be Calculated

- **On the basis of this Living Income (LI) can be calculated**. LI/year = (Number of Adult earners * LW) × 1.1, whereby 1.1 is an additional 10% for investment costs. This percentage can be adapted to the specific situation. So a higher percentage can be used to enable the farmer to make use of items such as better seeds and better equipment. Additional investments needed to change to a more sustainable method of production may necessitate a higher percentage.
- Average farm size must be defined. Which average farm size is chosen depends on the chosen target group: marginal farmers or small farmers, fertility of the soil, mode of production, distance to the market.
- Production costs must be known for all products, including investment costs and depreciation. Even for one single crop these costs may differ, depending on method of cultivation, for example manual labour or use of tractors and other machinery, or with or without fertilizer and/or improved seeds. Also included in the production costs are rent payments to a land-owner or sharecropper: where part of the produce is taken by the land-owner. The amounts thus paid can be considerable.
- For fixed investment costs that must be made once in a couple of years, the amounts of depreciation can be used in the calculations. This applies also to livestock that is bought, then gives returns (milk) during a certain period and after that is slaughtered or sold. In this case the whole period of the life of the animal must be considered and the costs and revenues spread over the years.[2]

[2] Note that this is a very economic approach. Especially with pastoralists there are many other reasons to keep livestock, such as an investment for bad times, to be given as dowry and for status.

- Production per hectare must be known for each method of cultivation such as with/without fertilizer and/or improved seeds. The use of machinery can make a large difference.
- Additional income must be known, both from agricultural and non-agricultural sources.

Based on This Fair Prices Needed to Achieve Living Wages and Living Income Can Be Calculated

Fair Price

The minimum price the producer should receive in order to attain a living income is called the 'Fair' price. Here 'Fair' does not imply that a higher price cannot be more beneficial, but that any price below this fair price is not sufficient, and thus this is the absolute minimum price the producer must receive.

This price is based on the assumption of full-employment on the specific crop. In case the number of working hours is not reached over a year, we call the price the farmer has to receive in order to obtain a living income the 'Not-Fully Employed price.'

When we know the average size of the plots needed for full employment, all production costs and the living income, we can calculate the fair price for a specific crop.

Fair Price per kg = (total costs + Living Income – additional income) divided by production in kg.

Because production costs are different in each situation, there is also a different 'fair' price for each situation. This means that there is a different fair price for each mode of production.

The differences in the outcomes of living income calculations and actual income show the need to intervene in the market.

When there is a gap between income needed and actual income, the underlying reasons should be analysed. If a full-time working farmer does not receive the income for his/her crops that he/she needs for a 'decent life,' this is a reason to further analyse the pricing system in the production chain that the farmer depends upon.

Annex III contains an Excel sheet with the necessary steps for calculating a Fair Price.

CHAPTER 17

Case Studies

Abstract Cases are discussed in Malawi, Burkina Faso, Cote d'Ivoire and Cambodia. Should market or fair prices for labour be used in the calculations? In Malawi plot size is estimated to calculate a Fair Price. In Burkina Faso the Steele formula to calculate a Living Wage is used to arrive at Fair Prices. Here a differentiation is made between different modes of production. A Fair cocoa price is calculated for Cote d'Ivoire while for Cambodia the gap between Fair prices and market prices has been highlighted.

Keywords Malawi • Burkina Faso • Cote d'Ivoire • Cambodia • Calculation model fair price tea • 'Not-fully employed' price • Sorghum • Boucle du Mouhoun • Dédougou • Tea • Cocoa • Rice • Plough • Tractor • Poverty line • Seeds • Additional income • Not-fully employed price • Side-income price • Additional income price • Working days

Introduction

In this chapter a number of case studies will be discussed, namely in the tea sector in Malawi, the food sector in Burkina Faso, the cocoa sector in Cote d'Ivoire and the rice sector in Cambodia.

Attention will be given to the relationship between working days and the number of hectares needed for full employment. The chapter discusses

R. Bronkhorst, *The Economics of Human Rights*,
https://doi.org/10.1007/978-3-030-59166-3_17

the consequences of additional income and the absence of full employment for farmers, leading to different Fair and Not-fully employed prices.

Calculation of Fair and Not-fully Employed Prices in the Tea Sector in Malawi

Let us now look in more detail into the case of tea farmers in Malawi.[1] On average they have a plot of 0.6 hectares of which 0.4 hectares is used to grow tea and the remaining 0.2 hectares is used for maize and pigeon peas. As maize and pigeon peas can be grown one after another on the same plot within the same year, 0.2 hectares is used for maize and the same 0.2 hectares is used for pigeon peas. In order to be fully employed a plot of 1.39 hectares is needed, however: 0.93 hectares for tea, 0.46 hectares for maize and the same 0.46 hectares for pigeon peas. This leads to the following calculation for the Fair Price for tea (in Malawi kwacha, MKW) (Table 17.1).

Therefore, the total income at market prices is 116,714 + 27,476 + 8 1,083 = 225,273 MKW/yr.

> "A decent standard of living for a family of five is calculated from the updated living wage study by Richard and Martha Anker from July 2016.[2] This

Table 17.1 Fair price calculation for tea

	Tea	*Maize*	*Pigeon peas*
Ha	0.93	0.46	0.46
Yield/ha	7500	2500	900
Yield/kg	6950	1158	417
Price/kg	97.30	130	350
Revenue/ha	729,750	325,000	315,000
Revenues	676,235	150,583	145,950
Cost/ha	603,800	265,700	140,000
Costs	559,521	123,108	64,867
Revenue—costs	116,714	27,476	81,083

Source: Calculations based on data from Krain, Martin and Brill

[1] I am grateful to the authors Krain, Martin and Brill for their authorization to use the data they collected.

[2] Anker, M. and Anker, R. (2016), Wages Committee progress report 2016. http://www.malawitea2020.com/uploaded/2016/12/Malawi-Tea-2020-Wages-Committee-progress-report-2016-LR.pdf.

amounts to 1,132,257 MKW per year. If we assume that one household member works full time and another one dedicates 59% of his/her work time to productive work it will lead us to a work force of 1.59 people per household. Moreover, from the living wage study we know that a full-time tea worker is assumed to work 276 days per year. However, in our calculations we had to reduce the number of workdays by dividing this number by 1.12 which lead us to 246.43 work days per year because a tea farmer cannot make use of paid leave and sick days as this is possible for a worker employed on a tea estate. If we now divide 1,132,257 MKW by 1.59 and by 246.42 we will get to the amount that one work force must earn per day in order to reach a living income. The result is that an income of 2889 MKW per one work force per work day is needed to provide a household of five with a decent standard of living. (Krain, Martin and Brill)"

Living Income consists of the amount needed for a decent standard of living (1,132,257 + 5% investment costs), and thus Living Income for the household will be 1,188,870 MKW.

This means that the fair price for tea consists of the total costs of the production of tea plus Living Income minus net additional income, in this case the net income from maize and pigeon peas, divided by the total tea yield, or (559,521 + 1,188,870) – (27,476 + 81,083) / 6950 = 235.95 MKW/kg. The additional investments are needed to be able to increase productivity and to prepare for the consequences of climate change.

Schematic:

Fair price Tea Malawi				Amounts in MKW
		Needed hh income/yr		**1,132,257**
Average number of adult earners per hh		1.59		
			LW pp/yr (per earning adult)	**712111**
		Total working days / yr		246
		LW per adult earning family member per working day		**2890**
Size of the farm in ha		1.39		
Production (kg)	**Tea**			
	6950			
	Production costs (MKW)			
	Tea	**Maize**	**Pigeon Peas**	**Total**
Total production costs	559,521	123,108	64,867	747,496
On basis of this Living Income (LI) can be calculated		factor>	1.05	
*LI/yr= (Number of Adult earners * LW) x 1.05*				**1,188,870**
Additional income (MKW)	**Maize**	**Pigeon Peas**	**Total**	
Total additional	150,583	145,95	**296,533**	
FP/kg = (LI +costs- add income) / production	***235.95***			

Note that in this case for maize and pigeon peas, market prices are used because this is the additional income actually received. To calculate the fair price for a specific product, market prices of other products are used. As there is no non-family labour, neither the calculated living wages nor the wages actually received and paid are used for this calculation. Also included in this additional income are the quantities used for auto-consumption at market prices.

There are arguments pro and contra the use of market prices for labour instead of living wages. On one hand, one could argue that the existing situation must be considered, and not a hypothetical one. On the other hand, this is about the calculation of prices that guarantee everyone a decent income, and hence living wages should be included.

The same problem is faced when deciding about market prices to be used for additional income, or fair prices. Usually fair prices are only calculated for the main crops and not for secondary crops, which are often used for auto-consumption. Therefore, market prices for additional products are used in this case.

In the case of the Malawian tea grower, the farmer does not have 1.39 hectares, but only 0.4 hectares. Since there is no possibility to expand the area of farmable land, he/she will have to live off the produce of this small parcel of land. When there is no alternative employment, the farmer is forced to be idle for part of the year. Yet he/she must live and support his/her family. We can also calculate a price for the situation where he is unable to earn other income. In that case we arrive at a higher price than the above-calculated fair price. This price may be considered not realizable, but it is the situation the farmer finds himself in. It is this situation that may inspire policy makers to find solutions for this pressing problem.

In order to differentiate between the price a farmer should receive when working full-time and the price he/she needs to receive when working part-time we may call the price in the case of full employment the 'fair' price, whereas the price a farmer should receive when not working full-time can be called the 'Not-fully employed' price.[3]

We then get the following 'Not-fully employed' price (Table 17.2).

Total income based on actual market prices is 5038 + 11,860 + 35,000 = 97,240 MKW.

[3] In a previous publication (Bronkhorst 2018) I used the term 'survival price,' but there was criticism that this term was more an indication for the (extreme) poverty line instead of for being partially employed, so I decided to replace it with 'not-fully employed' price.

Table 17.2 'Not-fully employed' price calculation for tea

	Tea	*Maize*	*Pigeon peas*
Ha	0.4	0.2	0.2
Yield/ha	7500	2500	900
Yield/kg	3000	500	180
Price/kg	97.30	130	350
Revenue/ha	729,750	325,000	315,000
Revenues	291,900	65,000	63,000
Cost/ha	603,800	265,700	140,000
Costs	241,520	53,140	28,000
Revenue—costs	50,380	11,860	35,000

Source: Calculations based on data from Krain, Martin and Brill

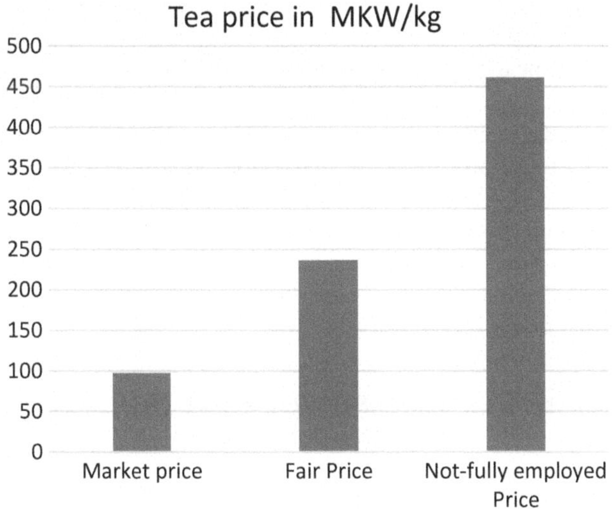

Fig. 17.1 Market prices, 'Fair' prices and 'Not-fully employed' prices for tea

With a Living Income of 1,188,870 MKW per year, the ***Not-fully employed price*** for tea will be.

$$\{(241,520+1,188,870)-(11,860+35,000)\}/3000=461.18\,\text{MKW}/\text{kg}$$

Figure 17.1 shows market prices, 'Fair' prices and 'Not-fully employed' prices for tea.

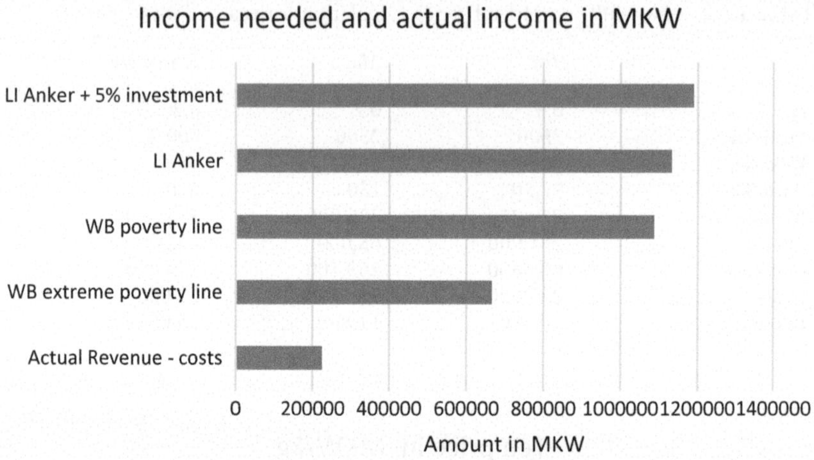

Fig. 17.2 Income needed and actual income in MKW

Coming back to the fair price, when we compare the actual income earned on 1.39 hectares with tea, maize and pigeon peas with the Living Income calculated and with the World Bank's Poverty Line of 3.1 US$ PPP and Extreme Poverty Line of 1.9 US$ PPP, this leads to Fig. 17.2.

What is very clear from the above is that it is impossible for the Malawian tea grower to reach a decent income with his/her actual production level and the actual prices received for the tea.

Calculation of Fair and Not-fully Employed Prices in Burkina Faso

In the previous example we have not considered different modes of production. This is done in the following example from Burkina Faso of grain-growing peasants. In this example we look at the effects on fair prices of the use of improved seeds versus traditional seeds and the use of a tractor against the use of a plough.

This is a simple example of the calculation of fair prices in a situation where not all data desired were present, and yet with the data available fair prices have been calculated.

Due to lack of an intensive survey of the target group, as in Anker and Anker's work, existing data had to be used. In this case the rural poverty line as calculated by the World Bank has been used as a benchmark.

Burkina Faso is a landlocked Sahelian country of 274,000 km^2 with more than 80% of the population living in the rural areas.

Forty-five per cent of the population has an income below the poverty line.

Sorghum, millet and maize are the main ingredients of the diet of the Burkinabè. In 2000–2002 these accounted for 66% of the total dietary energy supply.[4]

In Burkina Faso most producers are small farmers. WFP Burkina divides producers into small and medium-sized producers (90% of the producers) who produce limited amounts and may become net consumers in lean periods, and large-scale producers (10%) who produce significant amounts of tradable surpluses.

Of the small and medium-sized producers 56% is traditional agriculture and 34% works with draught animals. Only 10% of the producers are large-scale producers with mechanized agriculture (WFP Technical Meeting 2007).

There are three climate zones in the country going from south to north: Soudan, Soudan-Sahelian and Sahelian.

Our case study is the Dédougou region in the Boucle du Mouhoun in the Soudan-Sahelian climate zone.

In Burkina Faso there are two important agricultural methods of production: cash crops (especially cotton) and food products. One of the most important cereal-producing areas in the country, Boucle du Mouhoun, is an important producer of cotton as well. More than 30% of the households in this area receive a large part of their income from this source (CNCS/PNUD).

The greatest part of the production of cereals is auto-consumed by the producer families. Only part of this production is commercialized. The size of the production commercialized depends on the food security situation and the monetary needs of the family. According to CIC/B (Comité Interprofessionnelle sur les Céréales Burkina, a government organization representing the whole chain), farmers in the important production areas declared that the rise in cotton prices gave them the possibility of putting

[4] FAO Indicators BF.

more emphasis on the food security of the household at the expense of marketed food quantities. This was because revenues from cotton enabled them to pay the necessary monetary expenses and also to repay credits used to purchase inputs and equipment (Govt of Burkina Faso 2002).

According to Ruijs, a large part of the cereal harvest is consumed by the farm members and only a small part is sold.

It frequently happens that the same types of cereal are sold early in the season and re-bought a few months later (Ruijs).

Grain storage in Burkina Faso. (Photo by author)

Ducommun et al. found that in the Dédougou region in Burkina Faso, financial means are a very important constraint for the producers in that area. The main preoccupation of farmers interviewed was prices that are too low (Ducommun et al. 2003). They conclude that lack of financial means in the Dédougou region is a longstanding handicap to the growth in products traded (Ducommun et al. 2004).

In this region most of the households dispose of mostly archaic and inefficient agricultural tools. Inputs are little used and this prevents a rise in production. In their analysis of the causes of poverty in the Boucle du Mouhoun of 2004, it is stated that an average individual disposes of no more than 41,490 FCFA per year or 114 FCFA per day (0.23 US$). With this amount daily expenses of 248 FCFA (0.50 US$) must be covered (CNCS/PNUD).

As can be seen from the graphs below, sorghum is the food most produced, both in quantity and in surface used, in the Boucle du Mouhoun region (Figs. 17.3 and 17.4).

For the production of sorghum no fertilizer is used. The main differences in yield are the result of the use of tractor or plough and local or improved seeds.

Thus we can distinguish four cases:

1. Plough, local seeds
2. Plough, improved seeds
3. Tractor, local seeds
4. Tractor, improved seeds

For the calculation of the Living Income per family we start by taking the poverty line as the basis for our calculations (Table 17.3). Here we are faced with the problem that, although the methodology for calculating the poverty line is known, namely on the basis of costs of food and non-food,[5] different poverty lines exist, namely a national poverty line of

[5] From World Bank Report No. 29743-BUR: Box 4 How Is the Official Poverty Line Computed? "INSD (Institut National de la Statistique et de la Démographie) constructs a poverty line using the 'cost of basic needs' approach, in three steps:First, the food component of the poverty line is estimated by valuing a set of food items providing the recommended intake of 2283 calories per capita per day at the prices prevailing during the survey. The food items used by INSD consist of four staples most consumed by the households in Burkina Faso, namely sorghum, millet, corn and rice. A standard conversion table is used to determine the caloric content of each Kg of product. The composition of this food basket reflects the share of these four staples in the consumption of the households for each survey, and thus changes from survey to survey. The basket is evaluated at the prices of the four staples prevailing in Ouagadougou markets at the time of the survey.Second, the non-food component is equal to the non-food expenditures observed for the households whose food consumption is close to the food poverty line estimated above. The ratio of non-food to food consumption is estimated for each household. Then, the share of non-food consumption in the total poverty line is chosen to be the share reported by those households whose food consumption is close to the value of the food poverty line (for instance, ±1 percent). The ratio obtained thus far is multiplied by the food poverty line to get the non-food component of the poverty line. In other words if the typical household near the food poverty line consumes food and non-food items of about equal value, the non-food component would be set equivalent to the food poverty line.The official poverty line then is determined as the sum of the food and non-food components."

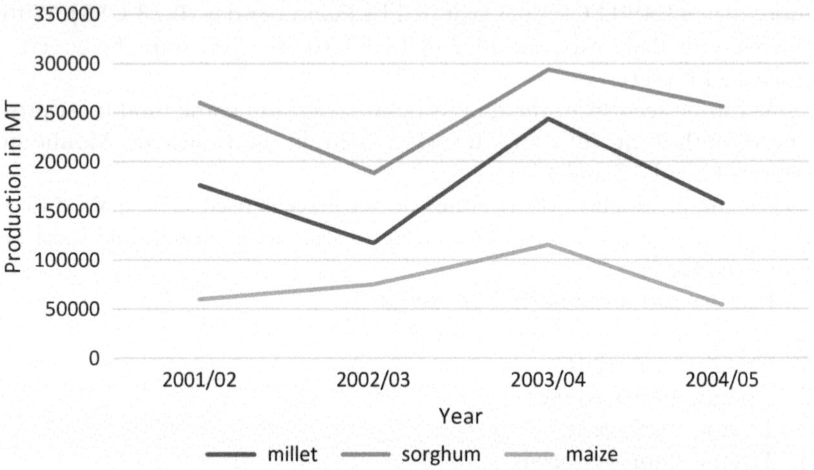

Fig. 17.3 Production of secondary cereals in the Boucle du Mouhoun region 2001/02–2004/05. (Source: Based on data provided by Direction des Statistiques Agricoles/DGPSA/MAHRH)

CFAF[6] 72,110, a rural poverty line of CFAF 71,737 and an urban poverty line of CFAF 73,557 (data INSD (Institut National de la Statistique et de la Démographie) in World Bank 2005).

For our calculations it seems appropriate to take the rural poverty line[7] as the point of departure because our case concerns the rural areas of Burkina Faso, Boucle du Mouhoun. This rural poverty line has been calculated at CFAF 71,737. This implies that in this case the Living Wage according to the Steele formula will be one that allows the worker an existence for him/herself and his/her family just above the poverty line. This means that they have enough food according to the standards as well as money for non-food expenses, in accordance with what is usual in this region. There is no guideline for what the housing should be as is the case of the Living Wage calculated by the Ankers.

The next step is to look at the average size of the family to calculate the Minimum Wage the worker should receive.

[6] FCFA stands for Franc CFA, the currency used in West Africa. It has an affixed exchange rate to the euro: 100 FCFA = 0.152449 EUR. An alternative term is CFAF.

[7] The high seasonality of prices of the main staples, especially during the lean period, contributes to the fluctuation of the nominal poverty line, and generates dramatic swings in the share of food in total household consumption from one survey to the other.

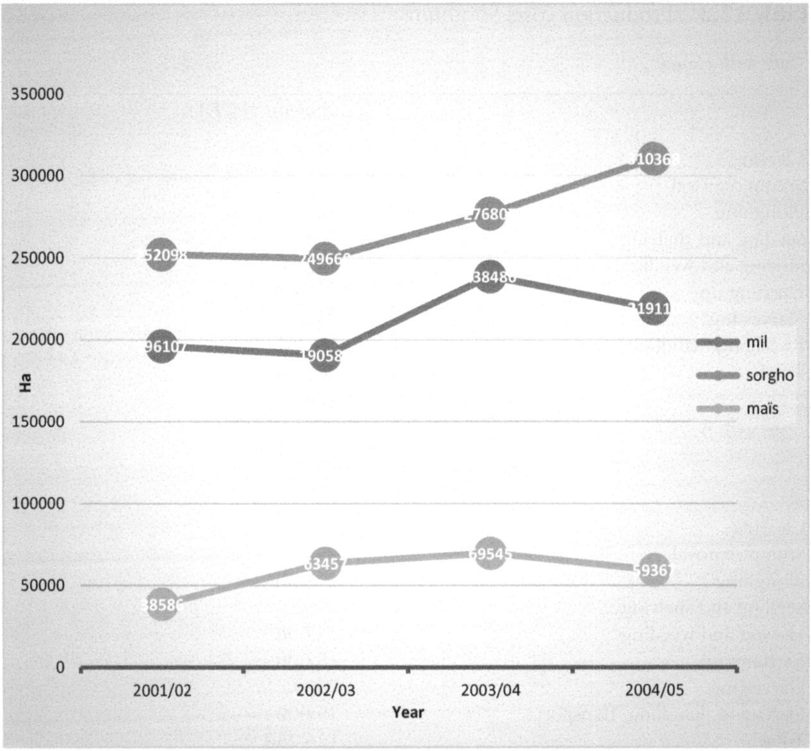

Fig. 17.4 Hectares cultivated in the Boucle du Mouhoun for millet, sorghum and maize. (Source: Based on data provided by Direction des Statistiques Agricoles/DGPSA/MAHRH)

According to the Burkina Faso household survey, 2003—SARPN, the average household size in 2003 was 6.4 (SARPN (Southern African Regional Poverty Network)).

ONAPAD estimates average household size in Boucle du Mouhoun at 7.8[8] (ONAPAD).

Since ONAPAD figures relate to Boucle du Mouhoun only, while the SARPN data are the average for the whole of Burkina Faso, it seems preferable to use for our calculations the data provided by ONAPAD, that is, an average household size in Boucle du Mouhoun of 7.8.

[8] A possible explanation for these large families given by ONAPAD is that many of the heads of the households practise polygamy (33.6%). ONAPAD is a cooperation between UNDP and the 'Ministère de l'Economie et du Développement' of Burkina Faso.

Table 17.3 Production costs Sorghum

Costs with plough

	Amount (FCFA)
Clearing	7500
Stump removal	7500
Ploughing	12,000
Seeding and shelving	3750
Hoeing and weeding	12,000
Earthing up	12,000
Harvesting	7500
Packaging, handling, transport	25,000
Total	87,250

Costs with tractor

	Amount (FCFA)
Clearing	7500
Stump removal	7500
Ploughing	25,000
Seeding and shelving	3750
Hoeing and weeding	25,000
Earthing up	25,000
Harvesting	7500
Packaging, handling, transport	25,000
Total	126,250

Source: Based on data provided by MARH Dedougou

In the case of African households, the wife works as much on the land as the husband. Children are also involved in agricultural activities in their spare time. Therefore both men and women between the ages of 18 and 60 are valued as 1,[9] and persons under 18 years as 0, as well as people of over 60 years.

For consumption purposes, though, children below 18 are counted as 0.5.

Akresh counts a number of 10.6 per household (Number of Members per Household 10.6, Number of Wives per Household 1.5, Children Under Age 18 per Household 3.6, Children Above Age 18 per Household

[9]This is different from the Anker approach. Anker values as adult workers those over the age of 25 years.

3.2 and Number of Additional Other Members per Household 1.3) (Akresh 2005), whereas ONAPAD counts 7.8 household members (ONAPAD 2004). Unfortunately, ONAPAD provides no details about the composition of the households.

If the percentages are equal in both cases, we can use the data to calculate the following composition of households in Boucle du Mouhoun:

Number of members per household	7.8
Head of the household	1
Number of wives per household	1.1
Number of children under age 18 per household	2.6
Number of children above age 18 per household	2.3
Number of additional other members per household	0.9

The total comes to 7.9 because of round-offs

Hence we may estimate the number of wage earners at 1 + 1,1 + 2.3 = 4.4,[10] and the size of the household at 1+1.1+2.6/2+2.3+0.9 = 6.6.

By applying the Steele formula, we arrive at a minimum wage required per adult worker of 71,737 (rural poverty line) * 6.6 (size of the household) = 473,464 + 10% (extra expenses) = 520,810.62 FCFA. When we divide this amount by the number of adult income earners who have to earn this amount (4.4) we arrive at a Living Wage for each adult worker of 118,366 FCFA per year.

To arrive at the Living Income we can multiply the Living Wage (118,366) by the number of adult workers (4.4) and add a certain percentage for farm investments. When we take a percentage of 10%, this means that the Living Income will be (118,366 * 4.4) + 10% = 572,892 FCFA.

[10] Reality is often more complicated than this. In addition to the fact that African men may have more than one spouse, there is often close cooperation between several households (brothers, sisters, parents) so that it is preferable to look at the Unit of Production and the Unit of Consumption to make a better calculation. For this example this would lead too far, however.

Schematically:

Family size	Head of HH	Wives per HH	Child < 18yrs	Child > 18yrs	≥ 60 yrs	Total	Amount in FCFA
Family members	**1,0**	**1,1**	**2,6**	**2,3**	**0,9**	7,90	
Weigh factor	**1,0**	**1,0**	**0,5**	**1,0**	**1,0**		
Weighed family members	1,0	1,1	1,3	2,3	0,9	6,6	
Cost of food pp /year							
Cost of non -food pp/ per year							
Total cost / year							XOF 473.464,20
				Needed savings	10%		XOF 47.346,42
				Needed hh income/yr			XOF 520.810,62
	Head of HH	Wives per HH	Child < 18yrs	Child > 18yrs	≥ 60 yrs	Total	
Average number of adult earners per household	**1,0**	**1,1**	**0,0**	**2,3**	**0,0**	4,4	
				LW pp/yr (per earning adult)			XOF 118.366,05
Working days/ yr = calendar days – Sundays – festivals – social obligations - calamities – sick days	*Total days/yr*	*Sundays*	*free days*	*sickness*	Total working days / yr		
Working days/ yr	*365*	52	20	18	275		
					LW per day		XOF 430,42
On basis of this **Living Income** (LI) can be calcula	factor>	1,1					
*LI/yr= (Number of Adult earners * LW)x 1,1*							XOF 572.891,68

What can be calculated now is the price the producer should receive for his produce to obtain a Living Income when producing sorghum only.

Separate prices should be calculated for each of the four cases:

1. Plough, local seeds
2. Plough, improved seeds
3. Tractor, local seeds
4. Tractor, improved seeds.

We can divide the peasants into roughly three groups. One group does not commercialize food, a second group does commercialize part of its produce, and a third group has a larger surface to work and commercializes part of its produce as well. All groups, however, may produce and sell cotton. The groups are defined according to the findings of the research done by TASIM/AO (Ducommun et al.).[11]

1. A group that does not commercialize food has an average of 2.8 hectares at its disposal.
2. A group that commercializes part of its produce has an average of 4.4 hectares at its disposal.
3. A group that commercializes part of its produce has an average of 6.8 hectares at its disposal.

[11] Unfortunately, TASIM/AO provides data at UP (production unit) only. UPs do not necessarily coincide with families. Due to lack of data at family level the data for UPs are used in the calculations.

The first group with an average of 2.8 hectares does produce food but this is mainly for auto-consumption and barter. They are outside the marketing system for food products (not for cotton) and therefore market prices of cereals do not affect them much. For our analysis of cereal market prices we therefore leave them out and concentrate on those peasants that commercialize (part of) their produce. Therefore we will discuss peasants with an average of 4.4 hectares at their disposal (Table 17.4).

In the case of a tractor plus local variety of seed, a total sorghum production of 5280 kg must be equal to 555,500 (costs) + 572,892 (Living Income needed) in order to achieve a Fair Price for the producer. This means the price to the producer should be (555,500 + 572,892) / 5280 = 213.71 FCFA/kg to achieve a Living Income (Table 17.5).

Table 17.4 Sorghum production costs and production in kg for 4.4 hectares

	Cost/ha (FCFA)	*Cost/4.4 ha (FCFA)*	*Production/ha (kg)*	*Production/4.4 ha (kg)*
Tractor and local variety	126,250	555,500	1200	5280
Tractor and improved variety	130,750	575,300	1700	7480
Plough and local variety	87,250	383,900	1200	5280
Plough and improved variety	91,750	403,700	1700	7480

Source production and production costs/ha: MARH, Seed price/ha FAOBF

Table 17.5 Fair Price for a kilogram of sorghum with tractor and local seed variety on basis of total production costs

Sorghum: tractor and local seed variety	
Total production costs	555,000
Living Income needed	572,891.68
Total production sorghum in kg	5,280
FP per kg = (costs + LI) / production	213.71

'Sorghum.'(Photo by author)

Table 17.6 Fair price for a kilogram of sorghum with tractor and local seed variety on basis of production costs per hectare

Size of the farm in ha	4,40 ha
LI/ha = Li/size of the farm	130,203
Sorghum: tractor and local seed variety	
Total production costs/ha	126,250
Living Income needed /ha	130,203
Sorghum production in kg per ha	1,200
FP per kg = (costs/ha + LI/ha)/ production/ha	213.71

When we make the calculation per hectare, we arrive at the same amount for the FP per kg (Table 17.6).

In applying this calculation to the other three cases as well, we obtain the following 'fair' prices for different cases (Table 17.7):

Table 17.7 'Fair' prices in case of 4.4 hectares sorghum only

	FCFA
Tractor and local variety	213.71
Tractor and improved variety	153
Plough and local variety	181
Plough and improved variety	130

Box 17.1 Relationship Working Days and Ha Needed for Full Employment

There is a relationship between labour available and the surface that can be taken into production in case of full employment. To be able to calculate a fair price we will consider a situation of full employment. Unless we assume full employment, we are faced with the situation of a fair price based on a hypothetical farmer possessing half a hectare where he/she works 60 days a year and the rest of the year is spent on something else, for instance another job. Then it would not be reasonable to assume that the income of the 60 days of work a year will provide him/her with an income that is sufficient to cover the whole year. In that case the additional income from the other job will also have to be taken into account in the calculation. Thus a fair price for a specific crop can only be calculated when we assume that all the farmer's time is devoted to this particular crop and all additional income is taken into account as well. This means that produce for own use (such as a vegetable garden, keeping chickens) must also be added to the income.

Full employment means that there are a certain number of working days a year. The total number of working hours should not exceed 48 hours/week and there must be spare time for expected and unexpected events, such as marriages, funerals and illness.

In the calculation examples we have estimated a number of working days per year, in the Burkina Faso case (above) 275 days a year.

These 275 days are calculated as follows (Table 17.8):

(*continued*)

Box 17.1 (continued)

Table 17.8 Calculation of working days per year

Total days/year	*365*
Sundays	52
Free days	20
Sickness	18
Total working days	275

This total number of working days of 275 days/year is the total number of working days for each adult member of the farmer's household. This number will be different for countries/regions because of cultural differences. In the Malawi example of tea farmers that discussed earlier, a total of 246 working days per year is assumed. The total working hours per year should not exceed the ILO Guidelines, however. In 1930 the general standard was set at 48 regular hours of work per week, with a maximum of eight hours per day. In 1935 the Forty-Hour Week Convention was adopted.

When a total of 1.8 hectares needs, for example, 200 days, then to fill the 275 days an area of 1.8 / 200 * 275 = 2.48 hectares is needed.

Hence where a total of 1.8 hectares needs 200 days, 2.48 hectares is needed for full employment in the case of one worker only. Is there a possibility to grow another crop to fill the missing 75 days? If so, then we obtain the total labour used to full employment. The additional crop can be valued at farm gate price as additional income. In case of other employment we can use the revenues from other work in the calculations as additional income.

In case of a 1.5 workforce (1.5*275 = 412.5 days), a surface of 412.5 * 1.8 / 200 = 3.7 hectares is needed.

These are the prices the farmer should be paid when the whole household (4.4 adult earners) is working all year on the production of sorghum only on 4.4 hectares.

It is important to note that these prices are only 'fair' prices when all available labour during the year is used for this purpose. So let us take a closer look at this.

When we look at our Burkina case of 4.4 hectares, it is doubtful whether this requires 275 (work days per person) * 4.4 (number of adult workers) = 1210 work hours per year.

Therefore we will expand our analysis with (1) the possibility of additional income (cotton, vegetable garden, other work) that fills the gap to full employment, and (2) the case that full employment is not achieved.

1. Fair Price and additional income of farmers

   (a) Large amount of additional income

Fortunately, peasants in Burkina Faso's Boucle du Mouhoun are not dependent on these food crops only; large amounts of cotton are also produced.

Suppose net household income from the cultivation of cotton amounts to 200,000 FCFA. Then the Fair prices will change, because net income to be derived from these food crops may be less. In the formula for calculating the Fair price an amount of 572,892 FCFA has been used (Living Income) to achieve a fair price.

Now we can decrease the 572,892 FCFA with the 200,000 received from other sources, and the amount then to be used in the formula becomes 372,892.

This has the following effects on the price for sorghum:

{Costs + (LI – 200,000)} / production = (555,500 + 372,892) / 5280 = 175.8 FCFA/kg (Table 17.9).

Table 17.9 Fair Price Sorghum in case of tractor and local seed variety and large amount of additional income

Sorghum: tractor and local seed variety + add income	
Total production costs	555.500
Living Income needed	**572.891,68**
Additional income	**200.000**
Total production sorghum in kg	5280
FP per kg = (costs+ LI - add income) /production	175,83

(b) Small amount of additional income

Let us now take a look at the case where there is some small amount of additional side income, such as a home garden or a cow. In this case full employment is achieved by the combination of working on the target crop and the work to achieve the side income. This leads to the following case.

Additional small income (chickens, eggs, milk, etc.) can be included at market prices. Hence when they sell and eat for, for example 1000 FCFA chicken, 2000 FCFA milk and 500 FCFA eggs at market prices, the amount of 3500 FCFA is deducted from the amount (the Living Income) that has to be earned from sorghum. The amount to be earned from sorghum becomes 572,892–3500 = 569,392 FCFA, or per hectare 569,392 / 4.4 = 129,407 FCFA.

'Keeping goats for additional income.' (Photo by author)

Table 17.10 Fair Price sorghum in case of use of a plough and improved seed variety plus a small additional income

Sorghum: tractor and local seed variety + small add income	
Total production costs	555,000
Living Income needed	569,392
Total production sorghum in kg	5,280
FP per kg = (costs + LI) / production	213.05

So taking into account this additional income, the FP calculation for sorghum with plough and improved seed variety plus a small additional income will be as shown in Table 17.10:

Hence these extra minor activities of the household do influence the FP for sorghum, but to a minor degree.

Another case is when the main income is not from sorghum, but from another source. In that case the main responsibility to secure a Living Income is with the other source of income. This may be the case where farmers grow coffee, tea or cocoa for companies to whom they sell. Since this it is the main part of their income, these companies are responsible for paying Fair prices for the coffee, tea, cocoa and so on that they purchase from the farmers. The price of sorghum may in this case be called 'Additional Income Price.'

2. Fair Price and no full employment of farmers

When there is no alternative employment, the farmer is forced to be idle for part of the year. Yet he/she must live and support his/her family. Thus, we can calculate a price for this situation as well: the situation where he/she is unable to earn other income. In that case we arrive at a higher price than the above-calculated fair price. This price may be considered not realizable, but it is the situation in which the farmer finds himself. It is this situation that may inspire policy makers to find solutions for this pressing problem.

In order to differentiate between the price a farmer should receive when working full-time and the price he/she needs to receive when working part-time, we may call the price in case of full employment the 'fair' price, whereas the price a farmer should receive when not working full-time can be called the 'Not-fully employed' price.

Let us now take a look at what happens if there is no full employment and only 60% of the labour force is used during the year. If that 40% is not filled with other productive work, the farmer must live on the income earned with 60% work. This means he/she will need to receive a higher price for the product, in this case sorghum, to arrive at a Living Income.

Prices needed to arrive at a Living Income from the part of the sorghum only when only 60% of the workforce is employed are given in the Table 17.11. Since 4.4 hectares requires full employment, 60% of the workforce can cover an area of 2.64 hectares only. This means that total production will also diminish to 60% of 5280 = 3168 kg.

Therefore the sorghum price needed to cover the Living Income in case of 60% labour only, will be for sorghum with plough and improved seed variety, 286.05 FCFA.

As mentioned previously, this price will not be called a 'Fair' price but rather a 'Not-fully employed' price.

As in the case of full employment, it is possible that the main income is not from sorghum but rather from another source. In that case the main responsibility to secure a Living Income is with the other source of income. The price of sorghum may in this case be called 'Side-income Price.'

Thus we have four different prices for four different situations, namely Fair Price, Not-fully Employed Price, Additional Income Price and Side-income price.

Table 17.11 Not-fully employed price per kg of sorghum with plough and improved seed variety in case of 60% labour only

Sorghum: tractor and local seed variety with 60% labour	
Total production costs	333,300
Living Income needed	572,892
Total production sorghum in kg	3,168
Not fully employed price per kg = (costs + LI) / production	286.05

Schematically the different prices are:

Full employment			
Income source	Main income	Additional income	Calculated price for sorghum
Sorghum	yes	no	Fair price
	Yes	yes	Fair price
	No	yes	Additional income price
Part-time employment			
Income source	Main income	Additional income	Calculated price for sorghum
Sorghum	Yes	No	Not-fully employed price
	Yes	Yes	Not-fully employed price
	No	Yes	Side-income price

Calculation of Fair Cocoa Prices.

The following case involves cocoa prices in Cote d'Ivoire. Here the necessary Living Income has already been calculated by other organizations, and therefore emphasis in this table is on the calculation of the Fair Price, or in the terms used by the authors the 'Necessary farm gate price.' In this case cocoa amounts to 74% of household income.

When we look at Cote d'Ivoire, the income from cocoa is $ 2809.14, of a total Household (HH) income of $ 3550.50. This means that $ 741.36 of the HH income comes from other sources. This leads to the following calculation of a Fair Price (Table 17.12).

In the chapter on Alternative Approaches (Chapter 23) it is explained how Fountain and Hütz-Adams arrive at a different Necessary Farm Gate Price by applying a slightly different approach.

Table 17.12 Fair price cocoa Cote d'Ivoire

Total production costs	1,868
Living Income needed	**5,448**
Additional income	**741**
Total production in kg	1,863
FP per kg = (costs+ LI - add income) /production	3.53

Source: Calculation on the basis of data from Fountain and Hütz-Adams

The Case of a Cambodian Rice Farmer

In Cambodia farms are characterized by the World Bank as small, medium or large. The categorization varies by the crop. For rice, small is below 1 hectare, medium is between 1 hectare and 3 hectares, and large is over 3 hectares (WB Cambodian Agriculture in Transition 2015).

The next example concerns a household in Prey Veng Trabek where wet rice is grown. It involves a household that grows 1.5 hectares wet rice and has no other sources of income. For household size and Living Wage data from WageIndicator are used (www.wageIndicator.org). The calculated amounts of Living Wage min per month are between 1,089,800 and 1,614,900 KHR (Cambodian riel). By taking an average household size of 1.8 working people, this means a needed Living Income per household of between 25,893,648 and 38,370,024 KHR per year. One and a half hectares of land are used for the rice production, with a yield of 2500 kg per hectare. For the total of 1.5 hectares this amounts to 3750 kg. The number of working days per year is 250. This implies that the farming household should spend 1,8 * 250 = 450 working hours per year. In this case the rice production needs 75 days.[12] Therefore the price to be calculated is not a Fair Price but rather a Not-fully Employed Price.

The resulting Not-fully employed price per kg [(costs + LI - add income)/production] is then between 7262 and 10,589 KHR/kg. This is the situation where the farmer should be able to have a Living Income from his/her rice production only.

We can also calculate the price the farmer should receive when the income from the sale of rice should cover only the working days needed, leaving room for other occupations in the remaining period. In that case prices are considerably lower, namely, 1508 to 2062 KHR per kg.

Table 17.13 shows the calculations.

The rice grower would need 9 hectares to have full employment, which means that this is to be considered a large farm. In this case the Fair Price would be 1508–2062 KHR per kg.

Both Fair Prices and Not-fully Employed Prices are much higher than farm gate prices, which were 1250 KHR per kg. This shows that current prices make it impossible for farmers to achieve a Living Income with the production of wet rice only.

[12] The average number of working days required according to the WB report is 72. However, in this case a study by SOMO reports 75 hours.

Table 17.13 Calculation of not-fully employed prices in the case of a wet rice producer in Cambodia

Labour days	*120*				
LW min per month	1,089,800	Per year	13,077,600	Per working day	52,310
LW max per month	1,614,900	Per year	19,378,800	Per working day	77,515
Living income needed min	25,893,648				
Living income needed max	38,370,024				
Working days needed	72				
Labour costs min	3,766,349				
Labour costs max	5,581,094				
Own labour days min	75	3,923,280			
Own labour days max	75	5,813,640			
Number of ha	1,5				
Production cost/ha without labour	892,000				
Total production costs without labour	1,338,000				
Additional income	0				
Production wet rice/ha	2500				
Total production wet rice in kg	3750				
Not-fully employed price per kg min= (costs + LI - add income)/ production	7262				
Not-fully employed price per kg max= (costs+ LI - add income)/ production	10,589				
Since only 75 working days/year are needed, in these days 75/450 part of LI must be earned.			250 working days/year 1 person		
75/450 part of LI min	4,315,608		Family of 2	250*1,8	450
75/450 part of LI max	6,395,004				
This leads to the following *NFP min*	1508				
This leads to the following *NFP max*	2062				

Source: Calculations made on the basis of data from SOMO, WB and WageIndicator

CHAPTER 18

Summary Case Studies

Abstract Different approaches in different countries were used.

Calculation of fair prices must be addressed in a careful way. It is not easy to calculate a fair price for products that cover the whole region and all farmers. First it must be decided which concept of Fair Wage to use and which production costs are to be included in the calculations. Then there are large differences between regions in terms of soil fertility, rainfall, farm size, labour availability, level of technology, market access and so on, that make generalizations difficult.

The calculated 'Fair Price' will be higher when the Anker Living Wage is used than when a poverty line is used. In both cases all production costs are covered, as well as the payment of wages. The only difference is that the base upon which the calculations are made is lower when using poverty lines. The use of the Living Wage is to be preferred above the use of a poverty line, because the Living Wage gives the worker the possibility to lead a decent life, instead of just surviving as in the case of the poverty line.

In the two cases of India and Burkina Faso, the poverty line has been used as an approximate to Living Wages and Living Income in order to calculate Fair Wages and Fair Prices. This means that in these cases the Fair Price does not cover what is needed for Living Wages and Living Income as defined in Chap. 3, but leads to the amount that is needed to end above the poverty line.

R. Bronkhorst, *The Economics of Human Rights*,
https://doi.org/10.1007/978-3-030-59166-3_18

Keywords India • Malawi • Burkina Faso • Cambodia • Cote d'Ivoire • Cocoa • Rice • Sorghum • Tea • Excess costs

What we have seen in these case studies are different approaches in different countries.

The first case, in India, was about the calculation from poverty line via Living Wages to Fair Prices. This calculation was made on the basis of poverty lines, average household sizes and labour force participation rates. No data were available about the exact family composition such as number of children with their age, and thus calculations for the Living Wage were made on the basis of one (in the text) and one and a half income earner(s) per household (in Annex II).

In the case of Malawi we compared plots of 0.4 and 1.39 hectares in order to calculate the Fair Price, whereby the plot of 1.39 hectares requires full employment and the plot of 0.4 hectares leaves time for other activities, which means in practice mostly being idle because there are no or few and insufficient alternatives. This is why we call the required price on the plot of 1.39 hectares the Fair price, while the required price to arrive at a decent income for the family at a plot of 0.4 hectares is called the Not-fully employed price.

In the Burkina Faso case we have examined a scenario of 4.4 hectares of sorghum for various modes of production, namely with the use of improved seeds vs traditional seeds and the use of a tractor compared with the use of a plough. Here we found that there exist as many different Fair and Not-fully employed prices as there are cases, showing both the strength (namely that Fair prices can be calculated for each product and every case) and the weaknesses of the approach (the great diversity in fair prices, and hence it will be very difficult to calculate a fair price for a given product for a whole region). In addition, we defined an Additional Income Price in the case of full employment and a Side-income price in the case of part-time employment.

For Cambodia the case of a medium surface rice farmer was examined. Because there is no full employment the calculated price is a Not-fully employed price. The difference from the actual market price shows that it is impossible to earn a Living Income in these circumstances. The rice grower would need 9 hectares to have full employment. The resulting Fair Price is still much higher than actual farm gate prices.

In the two cases of India and Burkina Faso, the poverty line has been used as an approximate to Living Wages and Living Income in order to calculate Fair Wages and Fair Prices. This means that in these cases the Fair Price does not cover what is needed for Living Wages and Living Income as defined in Chap. 3, but with the use of the formula for Living Wage originating from Steele (ETI) it leads to the amount that is needed to end above the poverty line.

Usually the Anker Living Wage calculated will be higher than the poverty lines, be it World Bank poverty line or national poverty line. According to Krain and Steffens, "the WB Poverty Line giving base to something that we would not call a LI, but rather a survival income" (Krain and Steffens).

The Living Income concept as further developed by the Ankers (see Anker 2017) is based on the costs of a 'basic but decent' life. This is done by calculating the costs of food, acceptable basic housing, other essential needs (such as schooling and health care) and a small margin for unexpected events (such as illnesses).

Therefore the resulting 'Fair Price' will be higher when the Anker Living Wage is used than when a poverty line is used. In both cases all production costs are covered, as well as the payment of wages. The only difference is that the base upon which the calculations are made is lower when using poverty lines. It is evident that the use of the Living Wage is to be preferred above the use of a poverty line, because the Living Wage gives the worker the possibility to lead a decent life, instead of just surviving as in the case of the poverty lines.

In reality, prices based on the poverty line are very often already a great step forward for the workers, while prices based on the Living Wage/Income are a further important step forward again.

When discussing the poverty line, we are talking about absolute minimum amounts to survive and not about the concept of 'fair.' When discussing 'fair' an ethical aspect becomes involved. At that moment we are not discussing only minima to survive and other criteria play a role as well. The outcome may be that wages are considered 'fair' when they are sufficient to take a family of three adult units of consumption above the poverty line, or when the Living Wage is paid, but it may be any other outcome as well (see also the Vaughan-Whitehead benchmarks, Chap. 4).

It should be made explicit, however, by all who talk about 'Fair Wages' what their definition of fair is, so that people can agree whether they call this fair as well or not. The same applies to prices: Where do you draw the line between costs that have to be included in the price? When should costs made be considered excess costs? In my opinion you cannot speak of excess costs in the case of a producer who could produce more efficiently if he/she had had the means to invest, but since he/she does not have the money to buy these tools, he/she has to work with the kind of tools that he possesses at this moment.

What appears from these case studies is that the calculation of fair prices must be addressed in a careful way and that it is not easy to calculate a fair price for products that cover the whole region and all farmers. First it must be decided which concept of Fair Wage to use and which production costs are to be included in the calculations. Then there are large differences between regions in terms of soil fertility, rainfall, farm size, labour availability, level of technology, market access and so on that make generalizations difficult. To arrive at a Fair price for a certain product of a certain quality it is necessary to make choices with regard to farm size and technology applied by the great majority of farmers under consideration. Only after these choices are made can fair price calculations start.

In the case studies discussed, calculated fair prices are given assuming that these remain stable during a longer period. In reality this is not the case. Production costs differ from time to time due to changing prices for inputs, the season, climate change and so on. Moreover, living income changes from period to period, in the short term due to changes in food prices as well as in prices of non-food products such as agricultural tools, and in the longer term also because of changing family compositions. Hence ideally prices of changes in both cost of living and demographic changes must be recorded. Then one can arrive at a fair price that fluctuates over time, just as market prices do. To follow these changes a great deal of work is required, but it is quite possible and should be done.

Another factor that should be noted is that we have not looked at the distribution of rewards within the household. In these cases it is assumed that this happens in a just way, but it would be worthwhile to look exclusively at the distribution of the benefits within the household. For example, in Africa women often must use their own money for food and the children, whereas men can use the money as they please.

A last point: To apply fair prices, agreement of stakeholders is necessary. This will lead to a series of negotiations between stakeholders. This is within one country, so let us in the next chapters have a look at what happens when external stakeholders are involved as well.

After this discussion of specific cases, in the next chapters we will analyse how actors and stakeholders can deal with fair prices. In Chap. 19 we will discuss export products, in Chap. 20 the role of governments and international organizations, and in Chaps. 21 and 22 socio-economic effects of the payment of living wages and fair prices.

Here a distinction must be made between effects on different groups in society. First in Chap. 21 the economic and social effects of the payment of Living Wages, Living Income and Fair Prices on Producers and Consumers are discussed. Chapter 22 follows with an analysis of the relationship between Fair Prices and other development issues, such as child labour, environment/climate change, Covid-19, food assistance and policy implications. The chapter also discusses the fact that policy is not only about economic efficiency.

Chapter 23 discusses important alternative approaches to pay a decent minimum wage to labourers and prices to producers.

Then in Chap. 24 a summary is provided of the effects of payment of fair prices in agriculture on different groups in society (small farmers, hired labour, community and region, consumers, employers, employment, environment and sustainability, and government budget).

The last chapter contains concluding remarks.

CHAPTER 19

Export Products

Abstract The next question is how companies that buy products from more countries and regions and that prefer to have standard prices for the consumers can deal with the problem of negative effects of the payment of fair prices to producers on their sales.

Consultations with government and stakeholders about obstacles in the chain should be organized to analyse the problem. Consensus in the chain between all stakeholders is necessary regarding the fact that a Living Income can, and must, be included in the producer price.

When groups of unions and cooperatives work together with other groups, both in and outside their own country, their bargaining power grows. To confront the monopolistic or semi-monopolistic power of multinationals it is important that farmers are united, both inside the country and with other farmer organizations in countries where similar conditions exist.

Keywords Exports • Stakeholders • Consensus • Cooperatives • Unions • Monopolies • Multinationals

The next question is how companies that buy products from more countries and regions and that prefer to have standard prices for the consumers can deal with the problem of negative effects of the payment of fair prices to producers on their sales. Companies not only have to deal with

R. Bronkhorst, *The Economics of Human Rights*,
https://doi.org/10.1007/978-3-030-59166-3_19

producer prices but also with government rules and taxes (think of government regulations of cooperatives, anti-trust legislation, export taxes as well as other taxes) and consumer preferences.

The complex problem of standardized prices is difficult to solve in one country already, but the problem is even larger when we look at more countries. This problem does not only concern large companies: organizations like Fairtrade International must also deal with it.

Also for export products it is important that the company or organization takes into consideration that prices should be based on real, actual costs. This means that the world market is not only the basis upon which the consumer price should be determined, but the reality in the field. As we have seen, Fair Prices are different from region to region, and this is the basis to work from. Not by giving a premium on the local producer price, but by paying the actual costs as well as Living Wages and a Living Income. At a later stage the different producer prices in different countries can be averaged, and in this way the company or organization can arrive at a uniform sales price, the same way as with other costs, such as transportation costs.

This may lead to a higher consumer price than the consumer is willing to pay. For the company it will be difficult to arrive at a decent consumer price. In that case consultations with government and stakeholders about obstacles in the chain should be organized to analyse the problem. Consensus in the chain between all stakeholders is necessary regarding the fact that a Living Income can, and must, be included in the producer price. When they come to a consensus nothing much changes for them, as companies already purchase for quality and profit reasons those products in those regions are the most beneficial for them. They only face an overall rise in production costs because of the payment of Living Wages and Living Incomes. When all companies agree to include basic workers' rights in their prices, they are all faced with the same problem. When only one company introduces fair wages, this company has the disadvantage of the first mover. Thus it is important that they are all aligned. When they become aligned, however, companies are faced with antitrust laws that can make it difficult to make binding agreements with one another. There are possibilities, though, when it is argued that the payment of fair wages is an advantage for society as a whole. When that argument is accepted, a reliable certification scheme will probably be needed to make sure that fair pay arrives at the right places. Paying a higher price for the same product than others do will also be possible when there is a difference in quality. In this way products distinguish themselves from the competitors. It is very important that the local government sees the importance of consensus as well and agrees to it, because the government can fix rules. These stakeholders' meetings can be organized by the companies themselves and by local governments or NGOs. Consensus can also be achieved in multilateral agreements.

When it appears impossible to arrive at a consensus and the price cannot be based on the living income, stakeholders should reflect whether it would not be better for the farmer to change to other crops or other sources of income. It is a challenge for both policy makers and producers to determine what other possibilities exist in the region for earning a decent income. This is a difficult exercise, because if other possibilities already existed in the region, many farmers would already have changed to other work that is more rewarding. The need to find alternatives is only more emphasized in this case.

A very important point is that, just as in the case of industrial workers who join labour unions, farmers unite in cooperatives or other forms of cooperation. A worker alone has no power; a group of workers does. The same is the case with small farmers; a farmer who wants a better price for his products won't achieve much, but when farmers are united in cooperatives they may achieve more. When these groups of unions and cooperatives work together with other groups, both in and outside their own country, their bargaining power grows. To confront the monopolistic or semi-monopolistic power of multinationals it is important that farmers are united, both inside the country and with other farmer organizations in countries where similar conditions exist.

CHAPTER 20

The Role of Governments and International Organizations

Abstract The government's aim in development should be defined. This will enable local governments to develop policies. Governments can play an important role in negotiations between companies and farmers' groups. They are in a position to mediate and, where necessary, pass legislation taking the overall interests of the nation into consideration.

International organizations with their international experience can assist local governments in their role as negotiators between companies and farmers groups.

Keywords Government • International organization • Policy • Negotiation • FAO • ILO • IFPRI

Governments face the same problems as companies that work internationally, concerning the question of how to deal with different fair prices. They have a different role and responsibility, however.

For governments it is difficult to decide on a uniform policy with all these different fair prices.

As we have seen, different farmers with different family sizes and different modes of production have different fair prices. In addition, each different type of farmer has different fair prices for the same product. When the fair price for rice is for one farmer 100 in local currency, and for another 150, how can a coherent national agricultural policy be developed?

R. Bronkhorst, *The Economics of Human Rights*,
https://doi.org/10.1007/978-3-030-59166-3_20

For a government to develop policy measures, the majority of the farmers working a certain area of land with a certain technique can be taken as the point of departure, for example sorghum cultivated with or without a tractor.

The government can develop policies for each category and decide on which category to focus attention. The government's aim in development should be defined. Will the focus be on maximum output now, or a stable output in the future, or on quality of life for the farmers and improving overall quality of life in the rural areas? Will the government take into account long-term developments such as climate change? In case it is the wish of the government to stimulate certain crops, the development of their prices should be carefully followed and action should be taken when necessary, to guarantee the minimum price for the farmer.

Following the need to pay Fair Prices because of Human Rights, governments can implement price policies in a country. It is clear that when differences in price levels exist between one region and another, and a uniform price level is required, someone has to pay for the difference. This can be done, for instance, by subsidies to farmers in the poorer regions: a transfer of wealth from one part of the country to another. Here the government has to intervene.

As explained above, governments can play an important role in the negotiations between companies and farmers' groups. They are in a position to mediate and, where necessary, pass legislation taking the overall interests of the nation into consideration.

International organizations can assist local governments in their role as negotiators between companies and farmers groups. Their international experience can be of assistance in looking for solutions for particular problems that may arise. Organizations like the FAO and IFPRI have an extensive knowledge of agriculture all over the world, while an organization like the ILO (International Labour Organization) is specialized in areas such as workers' rights.

Also in multilateral agreements, rules can be formulated about 'Fair' producer prices to be paid.

CHAPTER 21

Socio-Economic Effects in Agriculture of the Payment of Fair Wages, Living Income and Fair Prices

Abstract A distinction must be made between effects on different groups in the society. In this chapter economic and social effects on producers and consumers are discussed.

An important reason why small farmers do not grow more is their lack of investment possibilities. In other words, since they always need all their income for their family needs, no money is available for production-raising investments. In the case of fair prices however producers will benefit from a rise in income and, through multiplier effects, their whole region will benefit (e.g. suppliers of tools).

Consumers have to pay more. A number of measures are mentioned to prevent them paying the full price for the income rise of the producers.

Special attention is given to cash transfers and food security stocks.

Keywords Producers • Consumers • Farmer • Hired labour • Cash transfers • Food security stocks • Economic and social effects • Investments • India

In Part I of this book general effects of the payments of living wages/ income and fair prices were discussed. Here we will pay attention to additional effects in the agricultural sector.

A distinction must be made between effects on different groups in society. In this chapter we will discuss the economic and social effects on

R. Bronkhorst, *The Economics of Human Rights*,
https://doi.org/10.1007/978-3-030-59166-3_21

producers and consumers, while in the next chapter child labour, fair prices and the environment/climate change, Covid-19, food assistance, policy implications and efficiency are given attention. After that, we will look in more detail at the effects on small farmers, hired labour, community and region, consumers, employers, employment, environment and sustainability, and the government budget.

Producers

A critique that is sometimes voiced is that the system of fair prices leads to support for less productive farmers, and in this way prevents other farms from growing. The existence of very small farms may indeed prevent larger farms from occupying more land, but all alternatives should be considered, taking into consideration in which case total production is higher and which part of the population benefits. Is the majority of the population better off with large or with smaller farms?

An important reason why small farmers do not grow more is their lack of investment possibilities. In other words, since they always need all their income for their family needs, no money is available for production-raising investments. Thus in the case of fair prices, producers will benefit from a rise in income and, through multiplier effects, their whole region will benefit (e.g. suppliers of tools).

Payment of fair prices will provide a boost for a decent life and food security for the farmer and his family and stimulate sustainable agricultural practices. Within a country, paying fair prices to producers of food with high nutritional value will stimulate production of these food crops instead of growing cash crops. It depends on the government to what extent it will stimulate this change, because fewer cash crops may create lower government revenues.

In the case of hired labour, the producer will have to pay more to the workers, which will be made possible by the higher price received. For the workers an increase in wages is very important to enable them to attain a decent income as well.

In the case of food crops it is likely that higher prices without a corresponding increase in income for the net consumers will lead to an overall fall in demand for food products. Lower imports of food, or other forms of government intervention to support the local producers of food, may be needed in this case.

A problem that may arise, both for producers and for governments, is that higher producer prices are difficult to sustain, especially in the case of (formal or informal) open borders.

Consumers

Let us have a look at the effects on consumers of paying fair prices to the producers of food.

When we make a distinction in the population between producers and consumers it is clear that their interests do not always match. Not only is a great part of the population both producer and consumer, but a rise in price of a certain good may lead to more income for the producer and lower spendable income for the consumer. Therefore a decent income for the food producer may be ethically necessary, but isn't this intention upset by such a decline in spendable income for the consumer that the result is worse than the cure?

Consumers have to pay more. What can be done to ease their pain and prevent them paying the full price for the income rise of the producers?

- Analysis of the chain: are there excess profits or other problems in the chain? If so, action is needed to tackle these imbalances. However difficult to address this issue may be, unfair value distribution remains a very important obstacle for a better income distribution (see also Part I, Table 8.1) and may lead to higher consumer prices than necessary.
- Subsidies on food. An example of government subsidies is India, where food stores for the poor exist. A negative aspect of this is that the system is very vulnerable to fraud.
- Cash transfers to the needy.
- Security and intervention stocks. Food is stored to be used in cases of shortage and/or to regulate the market. A disadvantage is that this is capital that cannot be used for other purposes, and is subject to loss in quality and quantity (rodents).
- Exporting less food, leaving more food to the local population.
- Subsidies on agricultural inputs, such as seeds and equipment, to small farmers so that their production costs are lower and therefore so is the consumer price.
- Market regulation boards.

- Warehouse receipt systems. These allow agricultural producers to access credit by borrowing against receipts issued for goods stored in independently controlled warehouses. In this way producers are able to delay the sale of their products until after harvest, until a moment when prices are generally more favourable. Warehouse receipt systems can therefore mobilize credit for the agricultural sector and improve agricultural trade (FAO 2015b), leading to lower consumer prices.
- Credit. This is a very temporary solution and leads to a debt that must be repaid in the future, but it gives producers the necessary means for investments.

Most of these measures have their effects on government expenses. The government must invest to support the poor consumers and/or accept lower revenue from taxes.

To add to what has already been mentioned about food subsidies, two policies that are often considered in the policy debate are (1) a subsidy for prices and (2) a cash transfer. Cash transfers have many advantages over price subsidies. They are better targeted and therefore less expensive than a generalized price subsidy. They also preclude the introduction of price distortions.

Box 21.1 About Cash Transfers

The outcomes of an FAO report from 2015 prepared by Oxford Policy Management (OPM) and FAO on the results of cash transfers are interesting. According to the report, "CTs (Cash transfers) were most effective at improving agricultural productivity and increasing spending on agricultural inputs (e.g. fertilizer, seeds, etc.) in contexts where the primary constraint was working capital to buy inputs, rather than land availability. However, investment in agricultural inputs remained lowest where land was less available and spending on basic needs was a priority."

> Across countries, land-holding beneficiaries reported being able to hire labourers to work and increase the productivity of their land. CTs were most effective at improving agricultural productivity and increasing spending on agricultural inputs in communities where the primary constraint was working capital to buy inputs, not land availability.

(*continued*)

Box 21.1 (continued)

In terms of sharecropping, "CTs affected tenure arrangements for beneficiaries who already held land de facto or who owned land, by allowing them to reduce the amount of land they sharecropped out, as was the case particularly in Ethiopia.

With regards to the labour practices of beneficiaries, casual labour was an important income source for asset-poor households across countries. CTs generally enabled beneficiaries to reduce their engagement in casual labour (especially distress sale of labour) and use their time differently—notably, for many of those with land, to work productively on their own farms" (FAO 2015a).

Thus cash transfers made it possible for farmers to improve their standard of living and invest in agricultural inputs where lack of capital is the main constraint. For labourers they offered the opportunity to work their own farm instead of working as an underpaid labourer.

Box 21.2 About Food Security Stocks

Amartya Sen writes in his book *The Argumentative Indian* in the chapter "Class in India" about Food Policy and Hunger. He argues that in spite of India's rapid elimination of famine since independence, which he calls an achievement of great importance, the percentage of undernourished Indian children is 40–60%, as compared with a proportion of 20–40% in Africa.

He also discusses the accumulation of food stocks as resulting from the government's commitment to high minimum support prices for food grain. The subsidy has not resulted in low food prices, but in high costs of maintaining an unreasonable high stock.

He argues that although small farmers and peasants who sell part of their crop suffer from low food prices, higher food prices benefit rich farmers much more than the poor, because the poor also consist of casual labourers, slum dwellers and so on. He then argues that high food prices are not a pro-poor stance because they benefit poor farmers, but that the net effect is quite regressive on distribution (Sen 2005).

(*continued*)

Box 21.2 (continued)

I think that at this point he makes a mistake by jumping to a conclusion. The fact that the Indian government is wasting money by mismanaging the country's food stocks does not imply that the principle of paying farmers a decent price and selling food to the poor population at subsidized rates is wrong in itself. The fact should not be overlooked that small and very small peasants will be able to invest in their production capacities once they obtain more income. This will ultimately lead to higher production, lower production costs and ultimately lower consumer prices. Hence the controversy should not be that in practice some well-meant measures don't work, but about the question as to whether there would be a better food security situation for the Indian people if the Indian government were to better manage its food stocks and its policy of high producer prices and subsidized consumer prices.

CHAPTER 22

Fair Prices and Other Development Issues

Abstract In this chapter the relationship between Fair Prices and other development issues is analysed, issues such as child labour, environment/climate change, Covid-19, food assistance and policy implications. The chapter also discusses the fact that policy is not about economic efficiency only.

Important questions when developing a coherent agricultural policy are also discussed.

Concerning food assistance, the effects of food aid on prices at the local markets should be examined in more detail. The usual analysis that compares quantities of food aid with the total production in the beneficiary country is not adequate. What is needed is a comparison not with total production but with quantities marketed in the beneficiary country/region.

What should also be considered are the effects on the farmers selling to the food aid organization. Where local purchases are made for the provision of food aid, the fair price can guide the determination of what prices should be paid to producers in order to have optimal positive effects.

To enable policy- and decision-makers to make use of its results, three Fair Price Goals (FPGs) are formulated.

Keywords Child labour • Environment • Climate change • Covid-19 • Food assistance • Policy • Efficiency • Common Agricultural Policy (CAP) • European Union (EU) • European Economic Community (EEC) • USSR • responsibility • target group • Fair Price • Fair Price Goals (FPGs)

R. Bronkhorst, *The Economics of Human Rights*,
https://doi.org/10.1007/978-3-030-59166-3_22

In this chapter the relationship between Fair Prices and other development issuesis analysed, issues such as child labour, environment/climate change, Covid-19, food assistance and policy implications. The chapter also discusses the fact that policy is not about economic efficiency only.

Child Labour

According to a study done in India commissioned by the India Committee of the Netherlands (ICN) by Davuluri Venkateswarlu called "The Price of Less Child Labour and Higher Wages," the available data suggest that the rise in wages on cottonseed farms had a positive impact on reducing child labour. The incidence of child labour in the locations studied has decreased. According to the author, increased wages, due to the increase in procurement prices paid to the farmers, have played an important role in the reduction in the employment of child labour on cottonseed farms. One reason he gives for why seed farmers could not afford to pay minimum wages to the labourers is the low procurement prices by the seed companies. This is an example of how underpayments of adult labourers influence even child labour. Because of the pay rise the proportion of child labour to the total workforce on cottonseed farms declined from 57.4% in 2003–2004 to 29.8% in 2009–2010 (Venkateswarlu).

Fair Prices and the Environment/Climate Change

We have seen that different situations lead to different fair prices. These are based on actual circumstances. We can also look at what the fair price will be at a future moment in different situations. This way we can take into account factors such as climate change and desertification.

We can take into account a diminishing production in the future because of climate change and soil exhaustion. A recent report by Intergovernmental Panel on Climate Change (IPCC), "Land is a Critical Resource," sets out options to tackle land degradation, and prevent or adapt to further climate change (IPCC). Knowing the future change in fair price will be of great importance to all who are involved in rural development and agricultural production.

Suppose a farmer needs a Living Income of $1000. He grows rice and some other crops on 2 hectares, 1.5 hectares of rice and 0.5 hectares of other crops. His side income amounts to $200. Production costs are $0.40/hectare and rice yield/hectare is 3250 kg.[1] Based on this, the fair price will be $0.56/kg whereas the prevailing selling price is $0.47/kg. When yield/hectare diminishes because of climate change or soil depletion to 2500 kg/hectare, his needed Living Income will not change, but the resulting fair price for a kilogram of rice will go up to $0.61.

We know what the fair price should be in the actual situation with the given mode of production. This mode of production may or may not be use chemical fertilizer, for instance. Now we can also calculate what the fair price will be when the farmer switches to a different mode of production, for example to complete organic farming. The fair price may be calculated for both conventional and organic production methods. When the fair price for organic farming is higher than with conventional farming, the buyer could take this into account by paying the organic farmer the organic fair price. It is common policy already for consumers to pay more for organically grown food than for conventionally grown food. Thus the cost of a switch from conventional to organically grown food is clear, not only for the consumer but also for the producer. The farmer has to balance between short- and long-term interests. Will the switch to organic farming give more opportunities to sell at a higher price, or will the sales diminish? Which method of production allows him to continue in the future without being faced with the danger of exhaustion of the soil? And what will be the rewards in the long term as well as in the short term? Payment of a fair price for his actual production will enable the farmer to make a deliberate choice because he/she is able to pay for the necessary investments.

The same argument of being able to pay for necessary investments applies to the shift to a more circular economy.[2] A circular economy is

[1] Turkey Southeastern Anatolia (1996) O. Gaytancioglua and H. Sürek, "Input use and production cost in rice cultivation in Turkey," http://www.fao.org/docrep/x7164t/x7164t06.htm.

[2] According to Wikipedia, a circular economy is "an economic system aimed at eliminating waste and the continual use of resources. Circular systems employ reuse, sharing, repair, refurbishment, remanufacturing and recycling to create a close-loop system, minimising the use of resource inputs and the creation of waste, pollution and carbon emissions" (Wikipedia).

becoming an increasingly important subject in today's world, where focus on renewable sources is rapidly growing. Peasants often work in this way already, and now they must obtain the opportunity and means to continue to work in a circular way and make the necessary investments.

The outcome of the farmer's decision will have effects on the cost of living of the urban population and on the eventual longer-term export possibilities that may decrease. Therefore this knowledge is not only important for the farmer and the traders, but also for government officials.

A phenomenon that is often observed is that more land is taken into production at the cost of forests and pastures. For the farmer this may be a logical and sometimes even necessary step to take. What should be taken into consideration by policy makers, however, is to what extent this is an economically wise decision for society as a whole. In some areas, such as desert-bordering territories, rewards from agriculture may be lower than from pastoralism. This is one of the numerous cases where the interest of the individual may be different from the interests of society as a whole. When soils better suited for pastoralism are used for agriculture not only do the economic benefits for society as a whole diminish, but also a socio-cultural way of living (pastoralism) is destroyed. Therefore careful analysis is needed to assess the socio-economic costs and benefits for society as a whole and for different groups in particular. Not only economic considerations should play a role; environmental and social considerations may be at least as important, if not more so. Advance of new techniques or other ways of producing may imply the end of a specific socio-cultural lifestyle, with all its positive and negative consequences. The case of the rain forests in Brazil has attracted international attention because here large parts of the natural forest are burned for agriculture and mining. And since the Amazon forests are considered the 'lungs' of the world, the whole world is involved in the consequences of the policies of the Brazilian government. The list of stakeholders in this case is very long: from original forest inhabitants to animal life, from specific trees and plants to economic gains in the short and long term. Calculation of future fair prices of the region's products may provide a basis for a comparison between alternative uses of the land. If prices paid are on the level of Fair Prices, comparisons can be made with alternatives. Attention should be paid to the fact though that fair prices are only one of several criteria. Policy decisions must be made on the basis of other factors than economic considerations, such as ecology and social factors, as well.

When a certain product, for example cocoa, is more rewarding than other crops, farmers may be tempted to expand the cocoa territory, leading to deforestation. This can lead to both overproduction of cocoa and damage to the environment. This can be an undesired side effect when payment of fair prices concerns cocoa only, and for other products no fair prices are paid. Hence it is important to look at the whole picture.

Regardless of the price received, there is always a tendency for farmers to expand their arable territory in areas where there is a lack of suitable soils because of population growth. This phenomenon can be observed not only with forests, but also in territories such as the Sahelian countries where pastoralists have lost much ground to agriculturalists in spite of the fact that for the country as a whole it is often better, both from an economic and an environmental perspective, to use these marginal grounds for nomadic livestock-keeping instead of for agriculture.

As much as we can take into account a diminishing production in the future because of climate change and soil exhaustion, we must consider population growth as well. What will happen if family sizes remains as large as at present and what will happen when there is a tendency towards smaller families? The lack of arable land creates many problems and conflicts between different parts of the population. This is shown, among others, by the numerous conflicts between agriculturalists and pastoralists because both groups claim the same land, land where in the past they cooperated peacefully. An example of such cooperation is the land that was used by the agriculturalist to grow the crops, and then after the harvest cattle ate the remnants and thereby fertilized the soil. Now these two groups often compete for the same land. To complicate matters even more, disputes about territory often evolve into conflicts between different races, tribes and religions, though the main cause is socio-economic.

In the Indian state of Kerala, the Kerala Land Reforms Act of 1963 made provisions relating to the fixing of a ceiling on land holdings, abolition of the tenancy system and the assignment of proprietary rights to land to the cultivating tenants. The abolition of tenancy has resulted in massive redistribution of land rights, and therefore of income. But now there is a new problem, namely, that farmers who received enough land to obtain a decent living pass away, and their property is divided among their children. Each son inherits a small part which is not sufficient to feed a family. This is a case which shows that land redistribution, however urgently needed in many cases, can be followed by new problems when again the holdings are too small. This shows the urgency of some kind of population policy in those cases. Here again the calculation of living wages and living incomes can be an important tool for policy makers, showing what will happen through the continuation of existing policies while population growth, climate change and soil exhaustion are demanding urgent action.

Covid-19

The same way the Plague (Black Death) in the fourteenth century was transmitted through international trade routes, Covid-19 has spread because of the frequency of international contacts. All regions of the world are interconnected through trade and international tourism. The Covid-19 crisis has shown that producing in different parts of the world can disrupt entire economies. When export from one country has become impossible, industries in other countries suffer as well.

European countries have recently been shocked to learn that so many essential medicines come from China and India. This has led to a renewed discussion about the desirability of spreading production worldwide. These discussions may lead to less outsourcing and thus less income for poorer countries. What will be the effects of these developments on the workers? Will they retain their jobs or become part of the desperate masses without work and without food? The way the fashion industry has reacted to the Covid-19 pandemic does not bode well for the workers. Thousands of workers have been let go and sent home without their wages being paid, because the large American and European importers, faced by a stagnation in their sales, have annulled their orders and sometimes even refused to pay for goods already delivered. Therefore local employers cannot consider raising wages to Fair Wages, but they are glad already when they can retain (a segment of) their workers.

The United Nations Development Programme (UNDP) proposes a Temporary Basic Income to protect the world's poorest people, in order to slow the surge in Covid-19 cases. According to the UNDP, a Temporary Basic Income would give them the means to buy food and pay for health and education expenses (UNDP). This idea of a basic income is not new and is centred on civic well-being. When all workers are paid Living Wages and Living Income, though, there will already be a basic income for this category of people.

New international trade routes (new silk roads) are being constructed, but it is doubtful whether this will keep international trade at the same level as it is now.

Food Assistance

Another subject that needs to be discussed here is food assistance, both by UN organizations and by NGOs. It is a great step forward that food aid is often purchased locally nowadays, in a region close to the region of destination, instead of being imported from Western countries. The World Food Programme (WFP) is an organization that has responded quickly to criticism of its policies: it stopped shipping meat to meat-exporting Sahelian countries, and started purchasing grains locally instead of shipping grain from rich to poor countries. This local purchase within the region has been a very important step for economic development.

In this way surplus regions can profit from the food assistance to a neighbouring region. Local farmers are currently involved in the sale of their surplus production to the World Food Programme. Something more, however, can be said about the prices of the purchased food.

Calculated fair prices can be used by governments as a guideline to decide whether there is a need to intervene in the food market. In the case of food assistance, for example, the effects of food aid on prices at the local markets should be examined in more detail. That is, the effects of bringing more food on the market (the supply side) on both producers and consumers. Part of this analysis should be the long-term effects of imported food on the consumption of locally produced food, such as rice replacing secondary cereals. The usual analysis that compares quantities of food aid with the total production in the beneficiary country is not adequate. What is needed is a comparison not with total production but with quantities marketed in the beneficiary country/region. From that comparison it often appears that food aid has a greater impact on local markets than in the case where the comparison is made with production data only.

What should also be considered are the effects on the farmers selling to the food aid organization. Where local purchases are made for the provision of food aid, the fair price can guide the determination of what prices should be paid to producers in order to have optimal positive development effects on the region from which food is sourced.

In 2006 both the FAO and WFP argued that local purchase at higher prices from local farmers is not beneficial because payment of a higher price leads to less food available for the target group (FAO 2006 and WFP 2006).

Their opinion is that increased procurement costs would mean a transfer of WFP resources from the poorest of the poor to less poor farmers who produce a marketable surplus (FAO 2006). It should be realized, however, that the target groups in WFP initiatives like 'school canteens' and 'vulnerable groups' such as mothers and sick people are not chosen because of their individual poverty or the lack of access to food of their families, but because they belong to a special group, living in a structural food-deficit area. In food-deficit areas there is a difference in food availability, however, and the beneficiaries of these WFP initiatives are not by definition worse off than some producers in surplus areas.

The analysis of WFP 2006 and FAO 2006 assumes that a fixed amount is available for local purchase while the number of beneficiaries depends on the quantity of food that can be purchased. In reality, however, the number of beneficiaries is fixed. Based on the number of beneficiaries to be fed, a quantity of food or an amount of funds to purchase food is requested. If the amount pledged falls short, the WFP should ask its donors to increase its monetary contribution.

The point of departure should not be 'how much money is available and how many people can we feed for that amount,' but 'on the basis of our analysis we have come to the conclusion that so many people are in need of being fed and to do so we need that amount.' Then the responsibility is laid where it should be, namely with the donors. It is true that many donors are not keen to provide funds for local purchase, and hence lack of funds is a major problem. However, to conclude from this observation that the farmer must bear the consequences of this lack of funds is looking at things upside down (Bronkhorst 2011).

As noted above, the WFP has adapted well to changing circumstances and changing ideas about how food aid can have positive development effects aside from giving relief to food-insecure people. The WFP has greatly improved the development effects of its local purchases by introducing its Purchase for Progress (P4P) programme. Through this programme, the WFP—which itself has pledged to source 10% of its food purchases from smallholder farmers—encourages national governments and the private sector to buy food in ways that benefit smallholders (WFP P4P).

Unfortunately, market prices are still leading. Prices and quantities are negotiated directly with farmers' organizations, based upon market prices for similar-quality products on the open market (WFP Blog).

The WFP also restricts the prices it pays for locally procured food to below import parity regardless of type of supplier, unless a donor has specifically requested procurement from smallholder farmers as the primary objective, agreeing to the WFP paying a price above import parity (WFP P4P 2014).

Policy Implications

Now that the methodology of how to calculate Fair and Not-fully employed prices has been explained, the question arises as to how policy and decision-makers can make use of its results.

The calculated prices can be used as a basis for overall producer prices for specific products in a country or region. Policy makers can compare the Fair and Not-fully employed prices with market prices. When market prices are lower than fair prices, studies should be conducted to analyse the causes. Is the chain not well organized? Are some players in the market chain too powerful? Are prices negatively influenced by the imposition of taxes or by the absence of taxes?

With the calculation of living income and fair prices, it is clear what the minimum earnings for a farming family should be and what prices are needed to achieve this. Not only is the fair price at a certain moment important, but it is also important to analyse what can be done to bring the fair price down without the farmer paying the bill for this. Then all kinds of conventional interventions can be considered, from income support to better market facilities, training and extension, improved infrastructure, supply of better and cheaper inputs, and so on. These interventions do not obtain their goal, however, if they are not done together with the payment of fair prices. These fair prices may change over time in different situations, as we have seen. It should be noted here as well that "in practice governments systematically prefer not to increase food-crop prices but to subsidize farm inputs, such as seed, fertilizer and machinery, which are primarily used by large-scale farmers" (Leys).

For export products the world market is important, which leads to the question of how companies that buy products from more countries and regions and aim to have standard prices for the consumers can deal with this problem. As discussed in Chap. 20, companies not only have to deal with producer prices but also with government rules and taxes.

This is a complex problem to be solved in practice in just one country, but the problem is even larger when we consider more countries. This is the problem that not only large companies but also organizations such as Fairtrade must deal with.

Hence calculation of fair prices can serve as a wake-up call for policy makers in the sense that now the goal to be reached is clear. Not only is the goal clear, but also the way to achieve this, namely the payment of fair prices to the farmers, because fair wages and living income cannot be obtained without fair prices.

The decisions taken at policy level will depend on the political will and the importance attached to the development of the rural sector.

We can formulate the following *Fair Price Goals* (*FPGs*):

Goal 1. Payment of Living Wages to all workers and Living Income to all entrepreneurs
This is a responsibility of governments, business and private as well as public organizations. Every business and organization is responsible for paying Living Wages to their workers.

Goal 2. Payment of Fair Prices to producers
Here also every business and organization is responsible for paying Fair Prices to their producers.

Goal 3. Policy development to introduce legislation to pay Fair Prices both within a country and worldwide
Governments and International Organizations should take action to formulate and implement legislation.

Efficiency

Above we have discussed the problems involved in the payment of Fair prices to producers of export products. A similar problem exists when we look at fair prices for food products within one country or region.

In the 1950s, the European Union (EU), then still the European Economic Community (EEC), developed a system, the Common Agricultural Policy (CAP), to give subsidies to farmers. In the case of CAP subsidies, larger and more mechanized farmers benefited more than small farmers. A major challenge is how to avoid especially larger and more mechanized farmers benefiting and making sure that small farmers also benefit. If the aim of a subsidy is to support the smaller farmers, interventions should be carefully directed to them. Especially in poor countries with a less developed administration it is difficult to control to which group, larger or small farmer, a farmer belongs.

But in the end it is not up to the analyst to decide, but rather the politicians. The analyst shows what the minimum price must be to guarantee a decent livelihood, but it is up to the politicians to decide how to achieve the goal.

One of the effects of CAP was that farmers sold their farms and started working in industry instead. There were ample possibilities for doing this, so both farmer and industry benefited. Where the possibilities for switching to a job in industry do not exist, however, it is a different story. The difference between large and small companies is not a matter of economic efficiency only; social factors are very important as well. Farmers working on large estates are labourers and do not feel responsible for the company as they did for their own farm. The former USSR has been a good example of this. Labourers do not feel responsible the way owners do for matters such as deterioration of the soil, an important issue these days with regard to climate change and soil exhaustion.

Moreover, more capital-intensive companies need fewer laborers. Money that is gained in this way must be compared with loss of income for those who lose work. Measures must be taken to prevent this vulnerable group from paying the price for more welfare for the rest of the population.

But larger and more capital-intensive does not necessarily imply a larger output/hectare. There are numerous reports that show that small farmers have a larger output/hectare than large farms.

The IFPRI report "The Future of Small Farms for Poverty Reduction and Growth" gives many examples of studies that show a common tendency for larger farms to yield lower gross and net returns per hectare of land per year than smaller farms (Hazell et al. 2007). The USAID paper "Determinants of Farm Productivity in Africa" states that in Rwanda, compared to the largest farms[3] the smallest farms have three times higher land yields in value terms and use four times more labour per hectare. Regression results show a strong inverse relationship between farm size and the MVP (marginal value product) of land, and a positive relationship between farm size and the MVP of labor (Reardon et al. 1997). Van der Ploeg concludes that "peasant agriculture contributes more (just as it

[3] The 'smallest' quartile of farms in the study sample average 0.34 hectares, the 'middle' quartile 0.83 hectares and the 'largest' quartile 2.38 hectares.

potentially can contribute far more in the decades to come) to total agricultural growth and, consequently, to the provision of food than other mode of agricultural production. However, this only applies if, and when, sufficient space and means are available. If the required space and means are lacking, this potential for growth and increased supplies of food becomes blocked" (Ploeg van der 2014).

We must take into consideration not only total agricultural production, but also land availability and abundance or shortage of labour. Different situations require different solutions. An increase in total production benefits consumers because of lower prices in case of perfect competition, but does not necessarily benefit the farmers. Mechanization may lead to higher yields, but may lead to large numbers of small farmers and labourers being out of a job and lose their source of income. Therefore a rise in production should never be the only reason to stimulate certain practices, but at least as important is the right of the people living off the land, to obtain an income in line with the UN's Human Rights.

Thus there are several factors that play a role, both social and economic. Every situation requires a specific solution. Economic macro factors alone should never decide the choice. Social factors must be heavily weighed, and on the economic side not only macro-economic factors but also the specific economic situation of the target group must be analysed and taken into account.

Therefore important questions when developing a coherent agricultural policy are as follows:

- How to have a general Fair Price for different regions?
- Will a Fair price not lead to inefficiency with the farmers in richer areas? Or, will fairness not be contrary to efficiency?
- What is the choice concerning the most urgent goals for the country: total yield, high export revenues or a Fair income for all its citizens? Here a discrepancy may arise between the needs of other countries that require more food and other agricultural products at low prices for their populations, and the needs of the exporting country and its own population.

CHAPTER 23

Alternative Approaches

Abstract The Fairtrade approach to 'Living Income Reference Pricing' and its Fairtrade minimum price and premium are discussed. An important difference between the Fairtrade methodology and the Living Income/Fair Price methodology is that in the first case farmers receive a premium (a kind of charity) and in the second case they receive what they have a right to according to the commonly accepted 'Universal Declaration of Human Rights.' Attention is also given to the Cocoa Barometer approach which developed the 'Necessary farm gate price.'

Another very interesting approach is the Living Income Reference Pricing Tool methodology developed by Krain and Steffens, GIZ.

Keywords Charity • Benchmark • Cocoa Barometer • Reference price • Living income reference pricing • Fairtrade minimum price • Fairtrade premium • Living income reference pricing tool • Krain and Steffens • GIZ

In addition to the Living Wage/Fair Price approach there are also other methodologies that aim at fair prices, although often under a different name. Here we will discuss some of them.

All kinds of Fair Trade Organizations (FTOs) have done an important job by making the public and policy makers aware of the fact that producers often do not earn enough for their products. FTOs often work with

R. Bronkhorst, *The Economics of Human Rights*,
https://doi.org/10.1007/978-3-030-59166-3_23

cooperatives that they pay a better price than the market price. Then the cooperatives can decide for themselves to invest the additional funds in education, health care or any other purpose. This is different from the payment of a fair price to the individual farmer where he/she can decide what to use the additional money for. In one case the decision-making is with the cooperative; in the other case it is with the farmer. It is up to the farmers themselves to choose.

Unfortunately, not all cooperatives are set up by the farmers themselves. There are cases where it is the government that decides upon the creation of cooperatives. In these scenarios it can be doubtful to what extent the farmer finds him/herself represented in the cooperative.

The solution of the international fair trade movement to fair prices is prices consisting of a price floor combined with a premium (FLO).[1]

Box 23.1 Fairtrade on 'Living Income Reference Pricing'
A Living Income Reference Price indicates the price needed for an average farmer's household with a viable farm size and an adequate productivity level to make a living income from the sales of their crop. It is based on the following key parameters:

- Cost of a decent standard of living (Living Income benchmark);
- Sustainable yields (productivity benchmark);
- Viable farm size (to fully employ the available household labour);
- Cost of sustainable production (in order to achieve abovementioned yields).[2]

Note that Fairtrade takes into account an increase in productivity and the cost of sustainable production, instead of taking the actual, existing, situation as its point of departure.

Fairtrade Minimum Price and Premium

The **Fairtrade Minimum Price** is the minimum that producers are paid when selling their products through Fairtrade, and acts as a safety net when market prices drop. It aims to cover the average costs of sustainably

[1] Source: www.fairtrade.net.
[2] Source: https://files.fairtrade.net/2019_FairtradeLivingIncomeReferencePrice_Model.pdf.

producing a crop and acts as a safety net when market prices drop. Producers obtain the market price when this is higher and can also negotiate for more.

The **Fairtrade Premium** is an extra sum of money, paid on top of the selling price, that farmers or workers use to invest in projects of their choice.[3]

An important difference between the Fairtrade methodology and the Living Income/Fair Price methodology is that in the first case farmers receive a premium (a kind of charity) and in the second case they receive what they have a right to according to the commonly accepted 'Universal Declaration of Human Rights.' The Living Income/Fair Price methodology has been developed to calculate a so-called fair price for each crop on the basis of the methods of production that are most common in the region concerned. This to enable the farmer to earn a living income as well as to have financial resources for sustainable investments, and decide for him/herself about the use of the additional money. Therefore the responsibility of the individual farmer is central in the Living Income/Fair Price methodology. This does not take away the important role cooperatives can play for the farmers. Cooperatives can play an important role in matters such as negotiations with buyers, coordinating different activities such as storage and transport, and obtaining access to credits. What is important, however, is the freedom of choice for the farmer.

Cocoa Barometer

The following example relates to cocoa prices in Cote d'Ivoire. Here the necessary Living Income has already been calculated by other organizations, and thus the emphasis in this table is on the calculation of the Fair Price, or in the terms used by the authors the 'Necessary farm gate price.' In this case cocoa amounts to 74% of household income (Table 23.1).

While most current calculations for a desired farm gate price assume farmers will be able to significantly increase their productivity, here this is not the case. The authors speak of an 'Unrealistic Productivity increase':

> "All current calculations for a desired farm gate price assume farmers will be able to significantly increase their productivity. Only then will a family be able to earn a living income. There are several key problems to that approach.

[3] Source: https://www.fairtrade.net/standard.

Table 23.1 Necessary farm gate price cocoa

	Cote d'Ivoire
Total farm yield	1.863
Publicly available farm size	4.47
Production costs per hectare	$418
Total production costs	$1.868,46
Living income level per household	$5.448
% of household income from cocoa	74%
Gross income from cocoa necessary to achieve Living Income	$5.900
Necessary farm gate price per kilo	$3.166

Source: Fountain and Hütz-Adams

> First, earning a living income is a fundamental human right for everyone, and should not be available only to the highest achiever. Average cocoa farming households should be able to achieve a living income, not just the outliers. Second, it is highly questionable whether cocoa farms will be able to achieve the kind of productivity increase demanded by these calculations".

In addition, they mention the point that "farmers would have to invest money and labour to obtain and apply these inputs. This requires access to affordable credit, which is simply not available to most farmers presently" (Fountain and Hütz-Adams).

As mentioned above, they calculate a Necessary Farm Gate Price per metric ton of $3.166. The problem with this approach is that even when the farmer is paid the Necessary Farm Gate Price, he/she will not end with a Living Income. It is the price the farmer should receive to arrive at the cocoa part of the Living Income, but not attain a complete LI.

Chapter 17 explained that the Fair Price by applying the Living Income/Fair Price methodology will be $ 3.530 instead of $ 3.166. A Necessary Farm Gate Price of $ 3.166 is needed to fulfil the cocoa's part of the LI, but a price of $ 3.530 is needed to completely arrive at a Living Income.

The Necessary Farm Gate Price methodology undoubtedly is an improvement compared to the other approaches that take future yields into consideration.

Concerning cocoa, Fountain and Hütz-Adams recommend:

- Every chocolate and cocoa company, and every sustainability standard, should develop and publish a living income policy, including a clear statement on what the minimum farm gate price should be.
- Living Income Reference Prices should be based on the current reality of average cocoa farmers, not on hypothetical future yield scenarios for outlier farmers.
- Certification premiums should not be considered as a part of a Living Income reference price. (Fountain and Hütz-Adams)

Living Income Reference Pricing Tool

A very interesting approach is the methodology developed by Krain and Steffens, GIZ, explained in their handbook *Living Income Reference Pricing Tool.*

As assumptions they take full employment, the application of good agricultural practices and a fair intra-household distribution.

The Reference Price is defined by them as follows:

> A reference price is "the price that has to be paid per unit in order to provide a household with a certain income benchmark." "A reference price equals the benchmark times labor units (e.g. in hours, days) plus material costs (e.g. for seed, fertilizer) plus hired labor costs, and all this divided by the yield of the commodity that is produced," while *living income* (LI) is defined as "the net annual income required for a household in a particular place to afford a decent standard of living for all members of that household". (Krain and Steffens)

Reference prices for agricultural commodities based on benchmarks can be calculated by using the equation

$$Reference\ price = \frac{benchmark\ /\ LU * HH\ labor\ LUs + material\ cost + hired\ labor\ costs}{yield}$$

where LU stands for labor unit.

For them paying a reference price may not mean that a household can actually fulfil its basic but decent needs. This is only the case if the assumptions of full employment, the application of good agricultural practices and a fair intra-household distribution are fulfilled.

Thus they apply the same assumptions as we do concerning full employment and a fair intra-household distribution, but in contrast with the Living Income/Fair Price methodology an increase in productivity is taken into account. Hence here we have the same point of criticism as with the Fairtrade approach, namely that they do not take as their point of departure the actual existing situation concerning the farmers' lack of sufficient agricultural tools. And it is this situation that can be improved by payment of Fair Prices.

CHAPTER 24

Summary Effects Payment of Fair Prices in Agriculture

Abstract In this chapter effects payment of fair prices in agriculture is summarized with regard to small farmers, hired labour, community and region, consumers, employers, employment, environment, sustainability and government budget. Specific social effects are also discussed.

Keywords Effects • Small farmer • Hired labour • Community and region • On consumers • Employer • Employment • Environment and sustainability • Government budget • Social effects

Effects on Small Farmers

- More income, leading to greater food security and more investment possibilities. They can afford better and healthier food for themselves and their family, better treatment in case of illness, and schooling for the children.
- Better and healthier food and better medical care eventually leads to higher productivity.
- Because they can afford education for the children, there will be less child labour
- Schooling will provide children with knowledge of new basic production techniques, which they can in turn pass on to their parents.

R. Bronkhorst, *The Economics of Human Rights*,
https://doi.org/10.1007/978-3-030-59166-3_24

- The higher income will enable the farmer to invest in better and more sustainable production methods.
- It also gives the farmer (investment) tools to adapt to changing circumstances because of climate change.

Effects on Hired Labour

Labourers will benefit from higher income and because of this an improved food security situation.

Just as is the case with small farmers, this will lead to better access to health services and education for their children.

Investments by the farmers will lead to more demand for more highly-trained labour. On the other hand there will be less work for lower-trained labourers.

Labourers will tend to migrate to regions where higher wages are paid, leaving lower-paying farmers with lower-skilled labour only.

Effects on Community and Region

Higher food prices will usually lead to higher food production, and thus to more local food on the markets. At the same time it will make local food consumption more costly. Thus there are two different influences: a larger supply versus a diminished demand for locally produced food.

Therefore government policy concerning import and export is very important.

The higher spendable income of producers and less spendable income of consumers will have multiplier effects on both community and region. Rural shops as well as suppliers and transporters may benefit from the increase in purchasing power of the rural population, while the urban poor and urban shopkeepers will be worse off. Here again government policy becomes very important: To what extent will they let the urban poor bear the cost of improvement of the well-being of the rural poor?

Higher income for farmers and rural labourers will lead to less child labour since the family will be able to afford to send the children to school instead of having them work in the fields.

When conditions in rural areas improve, there will be less incentive to migrate to the cities.

The effects of migration because of growing wage disparities can be of great importance for a region. Regions where fair wages are paid will have a better educated and better paid labour force than regions where this is not the case.

Better education is not only important for the actual job they are doing; also when alternative possibilities appear, due to industrialization for instance, the chances of getting a better job increase.

Effects on Consumers

On the whole, consumers will be faced with higher consumer prices. Here we can distinguish between the effects of price increases on export products and effects of price increases on domestic food.

Export products:

Consumers in importing countries pay more, while the population in the exporting country is less directly affected. When higher prices in importing countries lead to lower demand, however, the effects on the local population may be in terms of employment possibilities, resulting in lower employment.

Domestic Food:

Marginal farmers will have more income from their production, but on the other hand they will have to pay more for the food they must buy. It depends on the individual situation of the marginal farmer whether the balance will be positive or negative.

Consumers who are non-producers are affected most: their purchasing power diminishes.

High food prices can be a great burden especially for the urban population. As mentioned previously, there are several possible solutions to ease the burden of high food prices for the consumer:

- Subsidies on food
- Cash transfers
- Security and intervention stocks
- Exporting less food, leaving more food to the local population
- Subsidies on agricultural inputs
- Analysis of the chain: Are there excess profits or other problems in the chain[1]?
- Market regulation boards

[1] The analysis should of course be followed by concrete measures.

- Credit. This is a very temporary solution and leads to a debt that must be repaid in the future.

It might be interesting to combine subsidies on agricultural inputs and credit with the important problem of sustainability. Subsidies and loans could be linked to the obligation to change to a more sustainable method of production.

Effects on Employers

Since the employer has to pay not only higher wages to the workers but also higher prices for the inputs when fair wages are paid here as well, the result will be that he/she is faced with higher costs.

Turnover and profits may diminish, but this depends on the elasticity of demand for his products.

In turn, the labourers working on the farm will be better motivated and they will be in better condition, and thus more productive. This will lead to higher productivity for the firm.

Since farmers and labourers are paid well, more labourers will be available for the work.

Not all employers will be able to pay higher costs, and thus they will be faced with the question of how to reorganize.

Effects on Employment

Higher income for farmers and rural labourers will lead to less child labour since the family can afford to send the children to school instead of having them work in the fields. This means that the demand for adult workers rises.

There will be a shift to better educated and trained labour at the expense of unskilled labour. It will also become more attractive to work as a labourer when the rewards are higher.

As stated above, more and better trained labourers will be available in regions and with farmers where fair wages are paid.

Effects on Environment and Sustainability

Payment of fair prices in itself does not have any environmental effects.

According to a study by Dennis Wesselbaum and Amelia Aburn, climate change is a more important driver for migration than income and political freedom at origin together (Wesselbaum and Aburn). Payment of a fair price can stimulate and enable the farmer to change to more environmentally-friendly methods of production and to prepare for climate change, because he/she will be able to make the necessary investments. Because of the additional income children can go to school and receive education on other production techniques.

The same arguments apply concerning sustainability: the farmer is better equipped to change to more sustainable practices. For policy makers it is important to analyse the long-term effects of the payment of fair prices on production and farmers' behaviour. They can take into account a diminishing production in the future because of climate change and soil exhaustion. Then its effects on fair prices and on the welfare of the population in case fair prices are not paid can be analysed.

Another effect that may occur is overproduction of certain crops when farmers receive a higher price and invest more. This possibility should be part of the analysis as well.

Effects on Government Budget

When exports diminish, the government will receive lower income from export taxes as well as from profit taxes.

However, the government will receive more income from income taxes in those countries where this is well organized.

Subsidies on food, security and intervention stocks, as well as on inputs and support to projects, all have negative effects on the government budget.

Hence in those cases where actual market prices are below fair prices, the effect on the government budget will be negative.

On the other hand, better nutrition and less child labour will lead to improved health and lower health costs.

Social Effects

Alongside all of the effects described above, payment of fair prices and living wages can also lead to other, more capital-intensive, forms of production, thereby destroying socio-cultural communities and ways of living.

This is also a very important aspect and should lead to the important question of what kind of society a country wishes to achieve in future. Not everything that is economically successful is for the larger benefit of the people in the communities. What is best for the benefit of the people cannot be decided on economic arguments alone. Arguments concerning tradition, customs, belief, social environment and so on play an important role in how people experience changes, but these are too often overlooked because they are not quantifiable. People tend towards extremism, however, when society changes too much in too short a period, and hence attention is required when changing to other production techniques and forms of cooperation.

Therefore, all effects should be carefully analysed in cooperation with the target group, whose wishes should weigh heavily, and not only economic effects should be taken into account.

CHAPTER 25

Concluding Remarks

Abstract Companies must know the minimum their labourers and suppliers should earn, to comply with their CSR obligations. To achieve Fair Prices for producers, Fair Wages for workers and a Living Income for farmers several steps have to be taken.

- In the field of economic theory the problem of fair producer prices has been ignored for too long. The focus instead has been on consumer prices, of course as important as producer prices, but the concentrated attention on consumer prices has taken away the attention for fair producer prices. Economists should address this challenge. This may require a paradigm shift from prices determined by the market, with all its flaws, to prices determined by needs, in line with the approach outlined earlier.
- In the field of basic human rights, it is important to realize that charity is something different than basic human rights. In many religions (Christianity, Islam, Buddhism, Hinduism) there is an aspect of charity, but receiving charity is different from receiving something you are entitled to. Even Fair Trade organizations have an aspect of charity in their method of pricing. This is shown by paying a premium above the market price, instead of recognizing that paying less than the fair price is a form of exploitation. The difference is that paying a premium implies a gift, while paying the fair price without any premium is paying the amount the producer and workers have a right to.

R. Bronkhorst, *The Economics of Human Rights*,
https://doi.org/10.1007/978-3-030-59166-3_25

- Payment of a fair price is not the solution to all problems connected with poverty and lack of food security, but it is an essential part.

Keywords CSR • UNDP • Anker • Fair Price Goals (FPGs) • Paradigm shift • Charity • Human rights • Religion • Covid-19 • Living Wage • Living Income • Fair Price • Prices Determined by Needs

It is confusing that the concept of 'Living Wage' is often not made concrete. This has led to many different methods of calculating a Living Wage. A Fair Wage is even more confusing, because it consists of more than a Living Wage alone; other aspects must be taken into account as well.

It should be kept in mind that Living Wage, Living Income and Fair Price are all normative benchmarks.

When calculating a Fair Price for a product it is essential that first the underlying concepts are clarified: how Living Wages, Fair Wages and Living Income are defined and calculated, and what production costs are considered usual and necessary in each situation. Only when these are clear can an answer be given as to what a Fair Price can be, given the underlying definitions. Therefore the Fair Price can be quite different when taking, for instance, a poverty line as a base for the Living Wage than when applying the Living Wage method of the Ankers.

As mentioned earlier, several methods exist to calculate Fair Prices and Living Income Reference Prices. Each person can use the approach that seems to him/her the most appropriate in their specific situation . In this book the 'Living Income/Fair Price' methodology has been highlighted.

To solve the problem of agricultural income that is too low to allow for a decent living, as well as to provide sufficient funds for necessary investments, it is important that the farmer gets sufficient revenue from his work to be able to achieve the following:

(a) to pay all costs, both fixed and variable;
(b) all workers get paid at least a 'Fair Wage' as well as the legal minimum wage;
(c) the producer earns at least a Living Income;
(d) the price is sufficient to guarantee continuity of the enterprise and make the necessary additional investments.

To determine whether this is feasible, the following steps must be taken:

- Choice of the target group (area, size of plot, family size, mode of production);
- Calculation of Living Income needed by the target group;
- Calculation of production, marketing, storage and other costs for the target group;
- Production of the target crop;
- Calculation of the price that will lead to a Living Income;
- Calculation of differences between Fair prices and actual market prices.

Knowledge of these items will enable governments to take those measures that are needed to formulate policies either to ensure a Living Income for the rural population through higher producer prices or to look for alternative measures to ensure at least Fair Wages for workers and a Living Income for farmers. Companies must know the minimum their labourers and suppliers should earn, to comply with their CSR obligations.

For farmers, especially small-scale and marginal farmers, it is important that they have sufficient income to cover all their essential expenses, as well as a surplus that enables them to invest in seeds and equipment, among other requirements. So the Living Income should be seen as the essential minimum a farmer should earn, including an increase by a certain amount to enable him/her to make essential additional investments.

Nowadays interesting initiatives are being taken to deal with the economic and social consequences of Covid-19. The UNDP proposes a Temporary Basic Income to protect the world's poorest people, in order to slow the surge in Covid-19 cases. According to UNDP a Temporary Basic Income would give them the means to buy food and pay for health and education expenses (UNDP). This idea of a basic income is not new and is very sympathetic. When all workers are paid Living Wages and Living Income, though, there is already a basic income for this category of people.

Also for full-time agricultural workers it is important that the differences between market prices and prices needed to achieve Living Wages are covered, so that employers are able to pay a decent wage to their workers in order to give rural people a chance to live and develop. One way to do so is by removing market distortions (such as subsidized food imports, food aid that is sold on the market, taking action against certain power positions in the marketing chain) that have a negative effect on market prices of agricultural products, as well as by providing infrastructure, giving income or production subsidies, and creating more remunerative employment in rural areas.

The decisions taken at policy level will depend on the political will and the importance attached to the development of the rural sector.

The following *Fair Price Goals* (*FPGs*) can be formulated:

Goal 1. Payment of Living Wages to all workers and Living Income to all entrepreneurs;
Goal 2. Payment of Fair Prices to producers;
Goal 3. Policy development to introduce legislation to pay Fair Prices both within a country and worldwide.

To achieve Fair Prices for producers, Fair Wages for workers and a Living Income for farmers several steps have to be taken.

- In the field of economic theory the problem of fair producer prices has been ignored for too long. The focus has instead been on consumer prices, which of course is as important as producer prices, but the concentrated attention on consumer prices has taken away the attention for fair producer prices. Economists should address this challenge. This may require a paradigm shift from prices determined by the market, with all its flaws, to prices determined by needs, in line with the approach outlined above.
- In the field of basic human rights, it is important to realize that charity is something different from basic human rights. In many religions (Christianity, Islam, Buddhism, Hinduism) there is an aspect of charity, but receiving charity is different from receiving something you are entitled to. Even Fair Trade organizations have an aspect of charity in their method of pricing. This is shown by paying a premium above the market price, instead of recognizing that paying less than the fair price is a form of exploitation. The difference is that paying a premium implies a gift, while paying the fair price without any premium is paying the amount the producer and workers have a right to.
- Payment of a fair price is not the solution to all problems connected with poverty and lack of food security, but it is an essential part.

Annexes

Annex I: History of Economic Thought

From Paper submitted to the 93rd Annual Conference of the Agricultural Economics Society (AES), University of Warwick, April 2019. (Bronkhorst 2019)

For Aristotle the just price reflected the labour that both parties put into their goods, and was just because the goods embodied equivalent amount of labour (Springer).

In the Middle Ages Thomas of Aquino argued that prices charged had to be just. A wage pushing workers below subsistence level eroded their chances of being virtuous and were therefore unjust. Thus, a moral economy needed to be balanced against the market economy through the cultivation of virtue.

Adam Smith (1723–1790), the most well-known classical economist, who is often quoted by neo-liberal economists because of the working of the so-called 'invisible hand', wrote in his best-known work 'Wealth of Nations': "No society can surely be flourishing and happy, of which the far greater part of the members are poor and miserable. It is but equity, besides, that they who feed, clothe and lodge the whole body of the people should have such a share of the produce of their own labour as to be themselves tolerably well fed, clothed and lodged" (Smith).

R. Bronkhorst, *The Economics of Human Rights*,
https://doi.org/10.1007/978-3-030-59166-3

The fact that Smith wrote this is important because it shows that Smith was also a 'moral' economist who did not take for granted that the invisible hand would solve all problems. He was in favour of freer trade that would remove restraints that lead to monopolies.

So it is good to realize that at that time already, the founder of economic science stated that the 'free' market is not the solution to all problems, and that the price determined by supply and demand does not lead to the greatest prosperity possible, unless all conditions are met, conditions such as absence of monopolies and the absence of great numbers of poor and miserable.

According to the classical economist David Ricardo wages, being the price of labour, have both a natural and a market price. "The natural price of labour is that price which is necessary to enable the labourers, one with another, to subsist and to perpetuate their race, without either increase or diminution", and

> The market price of labour is the price which is really paid for it, from the natural operation of the proportion of the supply to the demand; labour is dear when it is scarce and cheap when it is plentiful. (Ricardo)

Ricardo is of the opinion that the natural price of labour enables the labourer to keep himself and his family alive. When wages rise the number of children will increase, whereas the number will decrease when wages get lower. In case of a wage rise the supply of labourers will increase within a relative short period which will have as its consequence that wages will fall to the level of natural wages.

Marx refined the labour theory further with his distinction between exchange value and use value.

Neoclassical economics replaced the classical concept with an analysis of the equilibrium of supply and demand in a stationary state. They based a theory of the relative prices of commodities on the concept of utility. The price of a commodity is governed by its marginal utility, not by its usefulness. Where water is in plentiful supply, its marginal utility is low; where water is scarce its marginal utility is high, whereas in both cases its usefulness is undoubted. The marginal utility of diamonds is kept high by their scarcity.

Bentham measured welfare in terms of the ability to produce net pleasure. "Best" policy is one that produces the greatest overall utility. John Stuart Mill (1806–1873) writes in his "Greatest Happiness Principle" that

'Utility should be maximized by focusing on the general net happiness in society, calculated according to both quantities and qualities.' The benefits of markets should not be enjoyed on the basis of greater common good produced but on the basis of individual good (Wright).

Cambridge economist Joan Robinson criticized utility for being a circular concept: "Utility is the quality in commodities that makes individuals want to buy them, and the fact that individuals want to buy commodities shows that they have utility" (Robinson).

The criticism of John Rawls (1921–2002) on utilitarian ethic, is that it would never serve as system of justice that could bind people together. The extreme utilitarian (and economic) ethics examine only the *aggregate* welfare produced and has no concern for distribution or principles of justice (Wright).

Sen argues that there are three components that the evaluation of utilitarianism requires, namely (1) Consequentialism, all choices should be evaluated according to their results, (2) Welfarism, which limits the evaluation of labour in each case to the outcome of benefits, and (3) The highest total, adding them all without taking individual distribution into consideration (Levent).

Léon Walras further developed the marginalist approach by describing the economic system in general mathematical terms. Walras stated that for each product there is also a "supply function" that expresses the quantities producers will supply dependent on their costs of production, the prices of productive services, and the level of technical knowledge. In the market, for each product there is a point of "equilibrium" at which a single price will satisfy both consumers and producers. "'Marketing-clearing prices' ensure that all that is produced is sold. When the supply of a particular commodity is in excess of demand, however low the price, the price falls to zero—it becomes a free good. This rule also applies to labour. In a position of equilibrium, enough workers must have died off, at any time in the past when wages were zero, to make the remainder sufficiently scarce today to command a living wage" (Robinson and Eatwell).

About the state of equilibrium, it should be noted that the demand side consists of <u>effective</u> demand only, which means that the demand of people with no or little financial resources is not taken into account. So, the demand of the poorest is not taken into account in the equilibrium price. This is the case for all products, but especially for food products this is important since these are essential to survive.

Economics became more and more a mathematical instead of a moral science. At the time of the classical economists there was not yet such a strict distinction between economics, philosophy, and sociology as there is now. These sciences overlapped, so economics included a moral component as well. This moral aspect has been lost in the transition to modern economics which claims to be value-free.

There have been economists who have taken much more distance from the current neo- classical theory and have published serious criticisms of this theory. Here I will mention some of those critics who have taken into account more than only market equilibrium theories and have also introduced power relations in their studies.

Johan Galtung's ‘A Structural Theory of Imperialism’ has been influential, as well as Andre Gunder Frank's ‘Capitalism and Underdevelopment in Latin America’ (Frank). Galtung made the important differentiation between ‘harmony of interest’ and ‘conflict of interest’ between communities (Galtung). In Latin America, the ‘Dependencia’ theory was developed, with scholars like Prebisch, Furtado and Dos Santos. These theories argued that not alone there were relationships of dependency between the Center (the developed world) and the Periphery (the developing countries), but also between the centers and peripheries in both Center and Periphery.[1]

The idea of elites, national or international, that have their own interests which may be different from the interests of other parts of the population and may lead to bad institutions, has been worked out further by authors like Daron Acemoglu and James A. Robinson in their book ‘Why Nations Fail’ (Acemoglu and Robinson) and by Abhijit V. Banerjee & Esther Duflo who use the term “iron law of oligarchy” (Banerjee & Duflo).

[1] For more information on this subject, see Colin Leys ‘The Rise and Fall of Development Theory’

Annex II: From an Article in Economic and Political Weekly, vol. XXXIX no. 34, August 21–27, 2004 'Fair' Prices and Wages in India

Reprint of an article in *Economic and Political Weekly*, vol. XXXIX no. 34, August 21–27, 2004. https://www.epw.in/journal/2004/34/commentary/fair-prices-and-wages.html

'Fair' Prices and Wages in India

This paper is structured around some states and a group of workers that is often ignored, namely artisans in Delhi, Jaipur and Pondicherry. All these workers are working in the unorganised sector where trade-unions don't play a role.

Concerning general legal minimum wages exists in India a so-called 'floor level minimum wage'. The Second Labour Commission writes about this: "this floor level minimum wage may be treated as the current minimum wage".[2] This 'floor level minimum wage' has been fixed at Rs 1350.

Different general minimum wages have, however, been established for different states and unions. These are for Rajasthan, Pondicherry and Delhi as follows:

Table A.I Minimum wages state-wise in Rs per month

State	*Rs per month*
Rajasthan	1800
Pondicherry	1350 (floor level minimum wage)
Delhi	2709

Poverty Line

The poverty line per capita in India as defined by the Planning Commission is based on the number of calories needed daily per person. This quantity has been defined in 1968 by a Nutrition Expert Group and has been fixed at 2400 calories per capita in rural areas and 2100 calories per capita in urban areas. The difference in quantities of food needed in rural and in urban areas is due to the fact that living conditions in rural areas are more demanding. For instance, people have to walk great distances to have access to water.

[2] Govt of India: Report of the National Commission on Labour, pag. 1355

The quantification of the number of calories needed was after research translated into monetary units to answer the question: How much money is spent on average to achieve the necessary quantity of calories? Data for this came from an expenditure survey at the group involved. From this survey it appeared that, based on the actual consumer behaviour, in 1973–1974 on an average Rs 49.09 a month was associated with a daily intake of 2400 calories in rural areas, and Rs 56.64 per month with a daily intake of 2100 calories per capita in urban areas.

So, the poverty line defined this way is partly normative and partly behavioural. It indicates the monetary value needed to achieve the specific quantity of calories needed, taking into account the need for other, non-food related, expenses.

These amounts needed are adjusted regularly through follow-up investigations recurring at set periods.

Such a macro approach obviously meets with many objections such as that there are differences in calories needed between different occupations, differences between men and women, etc. When calculating an average such differences get lost. Other missing factors that should be mentioned include access to water, lack of possibilities for development, forms of discrimination etc.

In spite of the obvious disadvantages, in India the choice has been made for this approach, and we follow this choice in order to arrive at a practical system for calculating 'fair' wages. The amounts calculated for 1973–1974 have, based on follow-up surveys, regularly been adjusted during the years.

Life circumstances have changed too since 1973–1974, both in rural and in urban areas. Yet the official poverty line is still always based on these data and these data are adjusted to current circumstances. To compare: in 1993–1994 the adjusted rural poverty line, based on the consumption basket of 1973–1974 was Rs 206. But, since the consumption basket has changed during these years, according to Dev and Ranade this amount no longer supplies the quantity of calories needed. According to their calculations the real cost of sufficient calories is not Rs 206 (the rural poverty line), but Rs 320.[3] This would mean, when adjusted with the consumer price index for rural workers[4] the official rural poverty line in 1998–1999 amounted to Rs 310, whereas the poverty line according to Dev and Ranade should be Rs 481.

[3] S. Mahendra Dev and Ajit Ranade: Persisting Poverty and Social Insecurity, A Selective Assessment, in: Kirit S. Parikh (ed): India Development Report 1999–2000,Oxford University Press, New Delhi, 1999

[4] Manpower Profile India, Yearbook 2001, table 5.1.13

In this paper the amounts of the official poverty line are used, but it should be kept in mind that, following what has been said on this subject above, these amounts are rather too low than too high.

However, different amounts for the poverty line for different states have been calculated at an official level. This is because India is such a large country with so many regional differences.

Table A.2 State wise poverty lines for the year 1999–2000 in Rs per capita per month

State/Union Territory	*Rural poverty line*	*Urban poverty line*
Rajasthan	344.03	465.92
Delhi	362.68	505.45
Pondicherry	307.64	475.60

Source: Planning Commission, Government of India

The poverty line indicates an amount per month per capita. Not everyone within a household earns income, however. The following table indicates average size of households in Rajasthan, Delhi and Pondicherry.

Table A.3 Average household size by state/union territory 1999–2000

State/Union Territory	*Rural*	*Urban*
Rajasthan	5.6	5.0
Delhi	4.4	4.4
Pondicherry	4.2	4.0

Source: Manpower Profile India, Yearbook 2001 Table 1.17

The poverty line per household is obtained by multiplying the poverty line by average household size.

Table A.4 Poverty line in Rs per month per household by State/Union Territory

State/Union Territory	*Rural*	*Urban*
Rajasthan	1927	2330
Delhi	1596	2224
Pondicherry	1292	1902

Living Wage
The data concerning the poverty line and average household size can be used to calculate the 'living wage' according to the *1998 Living Wage summit formula*[5]:

$$\frac{\text{Average household size} \times \text{cost of basic needs per person}}{\text{Average number of adult earners per household}} + \text{savings (set at 10\% of income)}$$

The living wage is to be earned over a maximum working week of 48 hours and basic needs are defined as housing, energy, nutrition, clothing, health care, education, potable water, childcare, transportation and savings, though the possibility of including further need categories (e.g. entertainment, vacation, paid family leave, retirement, life insurance and personal liability insurance) is floated.[6]

In our case both average household size (Table A.3) as the cost of basic needs per person (poverty line) are known.

The 'average number of adult earners per household' however, is not so easy to obtain. Although many married women do have a paid job, this certainly does not apply to all of them. For cultural reasons, many women are not allowed to work outside the home. Where women, both married and single, are allowed to work outside the home, it often is only in places where the working place is considered 'safe' for them. The 'Labour Force Participation Rate' gives the following picture:

Table A.5 Labour force participation rates by State/Union Territory, 1999–2000

State/Union Territory	*Rural*		*Urban*	
	Male	*Female*	*Male*	*Female*
Rajasthan	50.3	38.8	49.9	14.1
Delhi	54.1	3.7	54.6	10.9
Pondicherry	58.8	29.4	57.4	18.1

Source: Institute of Applied Manpower Research, Manpower Profile India, Yearbook 2001, Table 2.2.2

Like all data, these should be carefully used. There is always the danger of drawing too many conclusions from data that cannot entirely be relied

[5] David Steele: The "Living wage" Clausule in the ETI Base Code, ETI, June 2000, p.6
[6] Ibid.

upon. What these data do indicate, however, is that many more men than women have a paid job.

What can indeed be concluded is that we cannot take for granted the fact that both man and wife have a paid job. This has its consequences for the calculation of the living wage. The outcome will be different when we make the calculation with 1, or with 2 income earners per household.

On basis of this it seems incorrect to make the calculation of a 'living wage' on the basis of 2 income earners per household. It seems preferable to calculate it on the basis of 1–1½ income earner per household.

This leads to the following quantification concerning the 'living wage'.

In case of 1 income earner per household.

Table A.6 Amount of the Living Wage per month in Rs by State/Union Territory in case of 1 income earner per household

	Amount living wage (Rs)	
State/Union Territory	*Rural*	*Urban*
Rajasthan	2141	2588
Delhi	1773	2471
Pondicherry	1436	2114

In case of 1½ income earner per household.

Table A.7 Amount of the Living Wage per month in Rs by State/Union Territory in case of 1½ income earner per household

	Amount living wage (Rs)	
State/Union Territory	*Rural*	*Urban*
Rajasthan	1427	1.726
Delhi	1182	1.647
Pondicherry	957	1.409

It is evident that the decision how many income earners per household to use for the calculations so as to arrive at a 'reasonable' minimum wage for the worker is a very important one.

The Committee of Secretaries of States in 1981 and the National Commission on Rural Labour in 1991 recommended that the minimum wages should be at such a level as to take a family of 3 adult units of consumption above the poverty line. When that advice is followed no further research into the number of income earner per household is needed.

The choice to be made here, namely, where to place the borderline, is essentially a political choice. That a clear choice is made, however, is important in order to avoid confusion.

Several alternatives concerning the minimum earnings per month have been calculated above for several states/union territories for the household to function at the level of the poverty line, both in rural and urban areas.

The following two tables put these results together.

Table A.8 Minimum amounts in Rs calculated per month for rural areas per State/Union Territory

State/Union Territory	*Poverty line*	*Living wage*	*Living wage*	*Proposal*
	Household	*1 income earner*	*1½ income earner*	*Commission*
Rajasthan	1927	2141	1427	1032
Delhi	1596	1773	1182	1088
Pondicherry	1292	1436	957	923

Table A.9 Minimum amounts in Rs calculated per month for urban areas per State/Union Territory

State/Union Territory	*Poverty line*	*Living wage*	*Living wage*	*Proposal*
	Household	*1 income earner*	*1½ income earner*	*Commission*
Rajasthan	2330	2588	1726	1398
Delhi	2224	2471	1647	1516
Pondicherry	1902	2114	1409	1427

These data are the result of different ways of calculating a bottom-line to wages that all give different results. As said before, a choice has to be made between several alternatives. This choice depends on what level of living can be agreed upon as being the absolute minimum. Here different choices may be made, and will be made, between say the Fair Trade movement and the management of a factory that barely succeeds in keeping the business going. Yet it is very important that the different actors, such as the Indian Government, the Fair Trade movement, trade unions etc. clearly define what in their opinion the absolute minimum is that workers need to live on.

Once the minimum is defined, it would be good to look at every firm separately to find out the situation of the workers with regard to how many people there are in the household, and how many adult income earners the household has. This, however, would result in different wages within the same firm for workers performing the same jobs.

As mentioned above, a practical solution to this problem is given in the recommendation of The Report of the Committee of Secretaries of States (1981), endorsed by a similar concept of three consumption units by The Report of the National Commission on Rural Labour (1991), that the minimum wages should be at such a level as to take a family of 3 adult units of consumption above the poverty line. This recommendation can be extended to the concept of 'fair' wages as well, in the sense that once a bottom line to the 'fair' concept has been chosen, 'fair' wages should be at such a level as to take a family of 3 adult units of consumption above the bottom line.

It should be kept in mind however, that the concept of 'poverty line' in itself has nothing to do with 'fair wages'. It is only used here as a 'tool' to be used in the calculation of fair wages. When discussing the poverty line, we are talking about absolute minimum amounts to survive and not about the concept 'fair'. When discussing 'fair' an ethical aspect gets involved. At that moment we are not discussing only minima to survive but will other criteria play a role as well. The outcome may be that wages are considered 'fair' when they are sufficient to take a family of 3 adult units of consumption above the poverty line, but it may be any other outcome as well. It should be made explicit, however, by all who talk about fair wages what their definition of fair is, so that people can agree whether they call this fair as well or not. Especially in the Fair Trade movement customers are attracted by the promise that the producer a fair price is paid (which implies fair wages to the workers) without anyone having defined how to calculate this fair price.

An additional remark should be made regarding home-workers and part-time workers. The amount earned during the hours worked should be divided by the actual number of hours worked and then multiplied by 48 (the maximum working week according to ILO-standards), so as to arrive at the income they should have earned had they worked that many hours.

Minimum Fair Price

Once a decision has been taken how to define and calculate 'minimum fair wages', we can relate the 'minimum fair price' to the 'minimum fair wages'. In this context it is important to remember the target-group, defined on page 1 of this paper, namely artisans. This often means smaller firms with few workers who are not organised in trade-unions. The fact that there are no trade-unions plays an important role in the sense that where those unions do exist, there is a different possibility for calculating 'minimum fair wages' as well. After all the unions are supposed to speak on behalf of their members and (should) know what the aspirations of their members are, and what they themselves consider 'fair'.

Apart from the legal minimum wages, firms should also pay their workers at least 'minimum fair wages'. These 'minimum fair wages' can be calculated with the aid of any of the methods described above, but they should be defined in any case.

After defining the 'minimum fair wages', we can proceed to the 'minimum fair price'.

The price the producer gets for its products should be such that:

(a) the price is sufficient to pay all costs, both fixed and variable costs,
(b) this price is sufficient to guarantee continuity of the enterprise,
(c) all workers get paid at least a 'minimum fair wage' as well as the legal minimum wage,
(d) the producer himself has an income that equals at least both the 'minimum fair wage' as well as the legal minimum wage,
(e) this price is sufficient to expand the business in a gradual way.

This leads to the following definition of 'minimum fair price':

> A 'minimum fair price' can be calculated in those cases where it is possible to calculate both production costs and 'minimum fair wages'. In that case the net price to be paid to the producer is at least such that continuity and development of the firm are guaranteed, while at the same time all workers get at least the local 'minimum fair wages' as well as the legal minimum wages.

Conclusion

Even in the absence of trade unions to protect the workers' interests, there appear to be several possibilities to define 'fair' wages and, following that, 'fair' prices. Although a lot of data are required to do so, it appears in India possible to find those data to calculate a minimum (the bottom line) for both wages and prices. This is also because so many data are already in the concept of 'poverty line'. These data can be taken as point of depart to calculate 'fair' wages and prices once the concept 'fair' has been clearly defined.

This makes it possible for all chains involved in the production process to calculate these minima themselves as well.

Annex III: Calculation Model for Fair Price

A1	B	C	D	E	F	G	H
2	**Annex III Calculation model for Fair price**				input		
3							
4	Family size	Head of HH	Wives per HH	Child < 18yrs	Child > 18yrs	≥ 60 yrs	Total
5	Family members						SOM(C5:G5)
6	Weigh factor						
7	Weighed family members	C5*C6	D5*D6	E5*E6	F5*F6	G5*G6	SOM(C7:G7)
8	Cost of food pp /year						SOM(C8:G8)
9	Cost of non -food pp/ per year						SOM(C9:G9)
10	Total cost per year	C8+C9	D8+D9	E8+E9	F8+F9	G8+G9	H8+H9
11					Needed savings	10%	10% * H10
12						Needed hh income/yr	H10+H11
13							
14		Head of HH	Wives per HH	Child < 18yrs	Child > 18yrs	≥ 60 yrs	Total
15	*Average number of adult earners per household*						C15+D15+F15
16						**LW pp/yr (per earning adult)**	H12/H15
17							
18	Working days/ yr = calendar days – Sundays – festivals – social obligations - calamities – sick days	*Total days/yr*	*Sundays*	*free days*	*sickness*		*Total working days / yr*
19	*Working days/ yr*						C19-D19-E19-F19
20							
21						***LW adult earning family member working day***	H16/H19
22							
23	On basis of this **Living Income** (LI) can b	factor>	1,1				
24	***LI/yr= (Number of Adult earners * LW)x 1,1***						H15*H16*D23
25							
26	Size of the farm in ha						
27	*LI/ha = LI / size of the farm*						H24/F26
28							
29	**Needed to calculate costs per crop / ha (these costs may differ, depending on way of cultivation,**						
30	**e.g. with/without tractor or plough and/or improved seeds)**					Sorghum	
31		a	b	c	d	a. tractor and local variety	
32	Investments / repayments (interest and depreciation)					b. tractor and improved variety	
33	Inputs					c. plough and local variety	
34	Hired labour					d. plough and improved variety	
35	Field operation costs						
36	Harvest and post harvest costs						
37	Transformation costs						
38	Storage, Handling and Transport						
39	Fertilizing						
40	Costs of the umbrellla organization						
41	Taxes						
42	Other						
43	Total production costs / ha	SOM(C32:C42)	SOM(D32:D42)	SOM(E32:E42)	SOM(F32:F42)		
44							
45	Production in kg per ha. per crop for dif	a	b	c	d		
46	Total production in kg						
47							
48	***FP per kg = (costs/ha + LI/ha) /production/ha***	(C43+H27)/C46	(D43+H27)/D46	(E43+H27)/E46	(F43+H27)/F46		
49							
50	***In case of Additional income***	a	b	c	d		
51	Home grown food						
52	Labour (working for third parties)						
53	Remittances						
54	Subsidies						
55	Other						
56	Total additional	SOM(C51:C55)	SOM(D51:D55)	SOM(E51:E55)	SOM(F51:F55)		
57	*LI - add income*	H24-C56	H24-D56	H24-E56	H24-F56		
58							
59		a	b	c	d		
60	***FP per kg =(costs + LI - add income) /production***	(C43+C57)/C46	(D43+D57)/D46	(E43+E57)/E46	(F43+F57)/F46		

Annex IV: Equations

We can ask how much money the farm should generate to be able to pay Living Wages if all adult workers work all year, full-time, at the farm. This implies calculations as to what crop should be produced with the given production methods on a certain type of land in a certain climate to optimize revenues. Revenues not only depend on quantities produced, but also on market prices. Quantity produced * price per unit – production costs – marketing and storage costs = revenue. Here it is mentioned that quantity and not quantity sold only because auto-consumption has to be taken into consideration as well. The sum of all Living Wages at farm level plus an additional percentage for farm investments will be called the Living Income (LI).

The size of this percentage depends on the prices of tools and inputs compared to cost of living.

Let us take a simple example of a plot of land of 1 hectare, with only one crop, for example wheat.

Equation 1

The revenues are: $X = a - y - s$.

Where:

X = total revenue
a = revenue at market price for wheat
y = production costs for wheat
s = marketing and storage costs

Production costs include depreciation costs on investments, as well as labour.

In order to be able to earn a Living Wage (LW), the following must be true:

Σ LW $\geq$ X, whereby X changes according to changes in the parameters a, y and s.

In Σ LW $\geq$ X a subjective element is introduced and Σ LW $\geq$ X is not necessarily always the case. Σ LW may be higher or lower than X. X is a certain amount and may be, or may not be, equal to Σ LW.

This implies that on the one hectare at hand, a certain sales price is needed to earn a Living Wage. Should we take an area of 2 hectare, though, the sales price that is needed may be different.

Therefore, the equation should be adjusted in order to take into account the size of the farm (Eq. 2).

Equation 2

$$X = \{(a * b * c) - (y * c)\} - (s * c).$$

Where:

X = total revenue
a = market price for wheat per hectare
b = production of wheat per hectare
c = size of the farm in hectares
y = production costs of wheat per hectare
s = marketing and storage costs per hectare

Extension of the number of crops to two, for example wheat and rice, leads to:

Equation 3

$$X = \{(a * b * e) - (y * e) + (d * f * g) - (z * g)\} - \{(s * (e + g)\}.$$

Where:

X = total revenue
a = market price for wheat per hectare
b = production of wheat per hectare
e = hectares used to produce whea
y = production costs of wheat per hectare
s = marketing and storage costs per hectare
d = market price for rice
f = production of rice per hectare
g = hectares used to produce rice
z = production costs of rice per hectare

This means that exploiting a fixed amount of land using given production methods, in order to arrive at a total revenue that equals the sum of the Living Wages, either prices must attain a certain level or other crops should be produced for which sales prices are higher. Decisions regarding which crops to grow in a certain year are routine considerations for farmers who have that choice. It is more complicated for those farmers who, because of climatic conditions and structure of the soil, do not have a choice between different crops. In the long run production methods that lead to higher yields may be introduced, but to do so the farmer first needs funds so that he can invest.

In reality marginal farmers live not only of their crops; they also have alternative sources of income (working as a day labourer, etc.). The equation then becomes.

Equation 4

$$X = \{(a * b * e) - (y * e) + (d * f * g) - (z * g)\} - \{(s * (e + g)\} + (q - h).$$

Where:

q = income from other sources
h = expenditure made to obtain this additional income

When the producer works alone, total revenue X should be at least equal to the Living Wage. But what if others are employed as well?

When there is question of hired labour, these costs are to be included in the production costs as actual expenses made by the employer. When, apart from net wages paid to the labourer, amounts have to be paid to pension funds, taxes and so on, these should be included as well.

In the case of his or her own or family labour, however, the calculation for family members' salaries for working hours should be equal to the wages per hour paid to hired labour (which in all cases should at least correspond with Living Wages for daily work during the whole year).

The outcome of the calculations of the adapted Living Wage formula must be compared with production costs. Using the equations above it is possible to calculate a price for the products for which the producer will be able to generate enough revenue for a Living Wage. This calculated price we will call a 'fair' price. The different 'fair' prices for different products must lead to a total revenue that has to be equal or more than the calculated Living Wage.

With this calculation we arrive at the Living Wage each worker should at the minimum receive for his work. At the level of the farm as an enterprise there is the obligation of a firm to pay Living Wages. Additionally, however, not only do wages have to be earned, but there also has to be enough surplus money to cover necessary investments.

Therefore, the amount to be paid on Living Wages (LW) should be raised for the farm by another say 10% to be able to invest in small equipment (hoes, shovels, etc.) and seeds as well. In this way we arrive at the amount needed to guarantee a Living Income (LI) to the farmer. Thus, $LI = \Sigma LW + 10\%$.

Literature

Acemoglu, Daron and Robinson, James A.: 'Why Nations Fail', Profile Books 2013.

Akresh, Richard: 'Risk, Network Quality, and Family Structure: Child Fostering Decisions in Burkina Faso', University of Illinois at Urbana-Champaign; Institute for the Study of Labor (IZA) January 2005, IZA Discussion Paper No. 1471; Yale University Economic Growth Center Discussion Paper No. 902 http://ssrn.com/abstract=643163

Anker, Richard: 'Estimating a Living Wage', ILO 2011.

Anker, Richard and Martha: 'Living Wage for rural Malawi with Focus on Tea Growing area of Southern Malawi', January 2014.

Anker, Richard and Anker, Martha: 'Living Wages Around the World', Edward Elgar 2017.

Asia Floor Wage https://asia.floorwage.org/.

Balaam & Dillman: 'Introduction to International Political Economy', fifth edition, Longman/Pearson, 2011.

Banerjee, Abhijit V. & Duflo, Esther: 'Poor Economics', eight impression, Random House India, 2011.

Basic: 'Who's got the power', 2014 https://fairtrade-advocacy.org/wp-content/uploads/2019/03/EN-Whos_got_the_power-full_report.pdf.

Bhorat, Haroon: 'A Tale of Two Impacts: Minimum Wage Outcomes in South Africa', 12/10/2013 https://blogs.worldbank.org/team/haroon-bhorat/rss.xml

Bronkhorst Ruud (2004): "'Fair' prices and wages'", *Economic and Political Weekly* vol. XXXIX no. 34, August 21–27, 2004 https://www.epw.in/journal/2004/34/commentary/fair-prices-and-wages.html.

Bronkhorst, Ruud (2011): 'How to strengthen the development effectiveness of local purchase for food aid', *Development in Practice*, 21:7, 2011, 913–929.

R. Bronkhorst, *The Economics of Human Rights*, https://doi.org/10.1007/978-3-030-59166-3

Bronkhorst, Ruud (2013): "'Fair' Prices: Peasants and the possibilities of a Living Income" (including a case study of Burkina Faso), InfoBridge, December 2013, https://infobridge.org/index.php/8-news/17-fair-prices

Bronkhorst, Ruud (2014): 'Towards an integrated approach for project analysis for small farmers: the Living Income / Fair Price method', InfoBridge, November 2014, https://www.researchgate.net/publication/307560414_Towards_an_integrated_approach_for_project_analysis_for_small_farmers_the_Living_Income_Fair_Price_method.

Bronkhorst, Ruud (2016): 'Guide How To Calculate Fair Prices', *InfoBridge*, 2016 https://www.researchgate.net/publication/310133756_Guide_How_To_Calculate_Fair_Prices

Bronkhorst, Ruud (2017): 'Fair prices to Achieve a Living Income', *Conference paper* XXVII European Society for Rural Sociology Congress, https://www.researchgate.net/publication/320101702_Fair_Prices_to_achieve_a_Living_Income.

Bronkhorst, Ruud (2018): 'Fair Prices to achieve a Living Income for Small Farmers and its relation to local food purchase programs', *Sociology and Anthropology* December 3rd, 2018 http://www.hrpub.org/journals/article_info.php?aid=7538

Bronkhorst, Ruud (2019): 'Fair Producer Prices', *Conference paper AES* (Agricultural Economics Society) Annual Conference 2019 https://www.researchgate.net/publication/332727083_Fair_Producer_Prices_AES

Carpio, Ximena Del and Nguyen, Ha Minh: 'The Unintended Consequences of Increases in the Minimum Wage', 04/25/2012 http://blogs.worldbank.org/allaboutfinance/the-unintended-consequences-of-increases-in-the-minimum-wage

CNCS/PNUD: 'Analyse des déterminants de la pauvreté dans la Boucle du Mouhoun', 2005.

Ducommun G, Cecchini H, Ouedraogo S & Bengaly A (2003): 'La commercialisation paysanne de produits vivriers, région de Dédougou'. TASIM-AO. Série « Documents de travail » No 1. Ouagadougou, Burkina Faso.

Ducommun G, Cecchini H, Ouedraogo S & Bengaly A (2004): 'La commercialisation vivrière paysanne au Burkina Faso, Synthèse des études régionales Dédougou, Fada M'Gourma et Kaya', TASIM-AO série « Documents de travail » No 6. Ouagadougou, Burkina Faso.

Ducommun G, Hugo Cecchini, Sylvestre Ouedraogo et Abdoulaye Bengaly (2005) : 'Rapport Final de Synthèse Commercialisation vivrière paysanne marchés urbains et options politiques au Burkina Faso', TASIM-AO.

ETI Base code: https://www.ethicaltrade.org/resources/eti-base-code

ETI 2016 https://www.ethicaltrade.org/resources/base-code-guidance-living-wages.

European Commission: 'Circular Economy Package Report: Questions & Answers', 2019. https://europa.eu/rapid/press-release_MEMO-19-1481_en.htm

FAO (2005): 'Commodity Chain Analysis; Impact Analysis Using Market Prices', Easypol Module 045, FAO. http://www.fao.org/docs/up/easypol/332/value_chain_analysis_market_prices_045en.pdf

FAO (2006): 'The State of Food and Agriculture, Food aid for food security?', FAO Agriculture Series No. 37.

FAO (2014a): 'The State of Food and Agriculture 2014. Innovation in family farming'. Rome FAO.

FAO (2014b): 'Food security indicators'.

FAO (2015a): 'Qualitative research and analyses of the economic impacts of cash transfer programmes in Sub-Saharan Africa', 2015.

FAO (2015b): 'Warehouse Receipt Systems' https://europa.eu/capacity4dev/sorudev/documents/warehouse-receipt-systems-fao-2015

FAO: 'Decent Rural employment.' http://www.fao.org/rural-employment/background/en/

FAOSTAT 2013 http://www.fao.org/faostat/en/#home

FLO (Fairtrade Int.). www.fairtrade.net.

Fountain, A.C. and Hütz-Adams, F.: 'Necessary Farm Gate Prices for a Living Income', 2019.

Frank, Andre Gunder: 'Capitalism and Underdevelopment in Latin America', Penguin Books Ltd., 1971.

FWF https://www.fairwear.org/stories/fwf-shares-knowledge-gender-panel-fta-conference

Galtung, Johan: 'A Structural Theory of Imperialism', Journal of Peace Research, vol. 8, No. 2, 81–117, 1971.

Gaytancioglua, O. and H. Sürek: 'Input use and production cost in rice cultivation in Turkey', 1996, http://www.fao.org/docrep/x7164t/x7164t06.htm

Gittinger, J. Price: 'Economic Analysis of Agricultural Projects', second edition, completely revised and expanded, Johns Hopkins University press, 1982.

Global Living Wage Coalition, 2013. https://www.globallivingwage.org/

Global Living Wage Coalition Joint Statement on Living Wage, 2013 https://www.isealalliance.org/sites/default/files/resource/2018-01/JointStatement_on_LivingWage_November_2013.pdf

Government of Burkina Faso, Ministère de l'Agriculture, Secrétariat Permanent de la Coordination des Politiques Sectorielles Agricoles (2002): 'Plan d'Actions sur les Céréales (mil, sorgho, maïs)', document final.

Government of Burkina Faso: MAHRH http://agristat.bf.tripod.com.

Hazell, P. and C. Poulton, and S. Wiggins and A. Dorward: 'The Future of Small Farms for Poverty Reduction and Growth' IFPRI 2020 Discussion Paper 42, 2007.

IFAD/UNEP: 'Smallholders, food security and the environment', Rome, Italy, 2013.

IFPRI: 'The Future of Small Farms for Poverty Reduction and Growth', IFPRI 2020 Discussion Paper 42 (2007).
ILO Declaration on Social Justice, 2008.
ILO Global Wage Report 2008/09.
ILO http://www.ilo.org/global/topics/decent-work/lang%2D%2Den/index.htm
Intergovernmental Panel on Climate Change (IPCC): 'Land is a Critical Resource', 2019. https://www.ipcc.ch/2019/08/08/land-is-a-critical-resource_srccl/
International World Union Confederation 'Scandal: Inside the global supply chains of 50 top companies', Frontlines Report 2016, https://www.ituc-csi.org/IMG/pdf/pdffrontlines_scandal_en-2.pdf
ISEAL https://www.isealalliance.org/.
Jaques, Nathalie June: 'Living Wage, Labour and Capital', MA Sociology Thesis, University of Auckland, 2015 http://hdl.handle.net/2292/26329
Joint FAO/WHO/UNU Expert Consultation on Human Energy Requirements 17 TO 24 October 2001, Annex 5: 'Energy costs of activities' http://www.fao.org/docrep/007/y5686e/y5686e0e.htm#bm14.5.
Kirwin, M. and J. Anderson: 'Identifying the Factors Driving West African Migration', West African Papers, No. 17, OECD Publishing, Paris, 2018 https://doi.org/10.1787/eb3b2806-en.
Krain, Eberhard and Martin, Friederike and Brill, Katharina: 'Living and Actual Income of Smallholder Tea Farmers in Malawi—Using a Fast-Track Method for Model Calculations', GIZ Working Paper June 2017.
Krain, Eberhard and Linnert Steffens: 'Living Income Reference Pricing Tool, A Handbook to Determine Reference Prices for "Agricultural Commodities Based on Benchmarks' (Draft), Deutsche Gesellschaft für Internationale Zusammenarbeit (GIZ), December 2019 (in preparation).
Levent, Adem. 'Economics and Ethics: Heritage of Amartya Sen', *Turkish Journal of Business Ethics*, November 2013 6(2) 123–133, https://doi.org/10.12711/tjbe.2013.6.2.020.
Levi, John and Havinden, Michael: 'Economics of African Agriculture', Longman 1982.
Leys, Colin: 'The Rise and Fall of Development Theory', James Currey 1996.
Living Income Community of Practice https://www.living-income.com/
Nadeau, Carey Anne and Glasmeier, Amy K.: n.d. 'Living Wage Calculator.
'User's Guide/Technical Notes 2018 Update 12/30/2018' https://livingwage.mit.edu/.
Nieuwenkamp, Roel and Hennis, Marjoleine: 'Scaling up Living Wages in Global Supply Chains', OECD 2016 http://oecdinsights.org/2016/04/28/scaling-up-living-wages-in-global-supply-chains/
OECD Guidelines for Multinational Enterprises 2011 https://www.globalbusinessandhumanrights.com/uploads/file/OECD%20Guidelines%20for%20Multinational%20Enterprises_2011.pdf.

ONAPAD: 'Analyse des déterminants de la pauvreté dans la Boucle du Mouhoun', Décembre 2004, ONAPAD—série études 8.
Pennycook, Matthew and Lawton, Kayte: 'Beyond the Bottom Line: The challenges and opportunities of a living wage', 2013 https://www.resolutionfoundation.org/publications/beyond-bottom-line-challenges-opportunities-living-wage/
Ploeg, J. D. van der: 'Peasant-driven agricultural growth and food sovereignty', *The Journal of Peasant Studies*, 41:6, 999–1030, 2014, https://doi.org/10.1080/03066150.2013.876997.
Reardon, T. and V. Kelly and E. Crawford and T. Jayne and K. Savadogo and D. Clay: 'Determinants of farm productivity in Africa: a synthesis of four case studies', USAID Technical Paper No. 75, 1997.
Ricardo, David: 'The Principles of Political Economy and Taxation', Everyman's Library, 1977.
Robinson, Joan and John Eatwell: 'An Introduction to modern economics', revised edition, McGraw-Hill, 1974.
Ruijs, A.J.W.: 'Cereal trade in developing countries: a stochastic equilibrium analysis of market liberalisation and institutional changes in Burkina Faso', University of Groningen, 2002.
ONAPAD: 'Analyse des déterminants de la pauvreté dans la Boucle du Mouhoun', 2005.
SARPN: 'Burkina Faso household survey', 2003 http://www.sarpn.org/documents/d0002933/16-Africa_dev_indicators_2007.pdf
SA8000 2014 http://www.sa-intl.org/
Social Accountability International (SAI) http://www.sa-intl.org/.
Social Accountability International (SAI): SA8000® Abridged Guidance–2008 Standard 32 February 2011, https://sa-intl.org/?s=SA8000%C2%AE+Abridged+Guidance%E2%80%932008+Standard+32++February+2011
Sen, Amartya (2000): 'Development as Freedom', First Anchor Books Edition, August 2000.
Sen, Amartya (2005) "The Argumentative Indian", Penguin Books.
Smith, Adam: 'Wealth of Nations', Wordsworth Editions Ltd 2012.
SOMO https://www.somo.nl/
Soto, Hernando de: 'The Mystery of Capital', Bantam Press 2000.
Spencer, Shawn http://slideplayer.com/slide/5308966/
Steele, David: 'The "Living wage" Clausule in the ETI Base Code', ETI, June 2000.
UN 'Universal Declaration of Human Rights' http://www.un.org/en/universal-declaration-human-rights/
UN Sustainable Development Goals http://www.un.org/sustainabledevelopment/hunger/
UNDP: 'Temporary Basic Income to protect the world's poorest people could slow the surge in COVID-19 cases', https://www.undp.org/content/undp/

en/home/news-centre/news/2020/Temporary_Basic_Income_to_protect_the_worlds_poorest_people_slow_COVID19.html
Vaughan-Whitehead, Daniel: 'Fair Wages', Edward Elgar 2010.
Venkateswarlu, Davuluri: 'The Price of Less Child Labour and Higher Wages', http://www.indianet.nl/ThePriceOfLessChildLabourAndHigherWages.html
WageIndicator www.WageIndicator.org.
Werner, Andrea and Lim, Ming: 'The Ethics of the Living Wage: A Review and Research Agenda', *Journal of Business Ethics* September 2016, Volume 137, Issue 3, pp. 433–447, https://link.springer.com/article/10.1007%2Fs10551-015-2562-z).
Wesselbaum, Dennis and Aburn, Amelia: 'Gone with the wind: International migration', Global and Planetary Change Volume 178, July 2019, Pages 96–109, https://www.sciencedirect.com/science/article/pii/S0921818118303308?dgcid=raven_sd_aip_email#!
WFP (2006): 'Food Procurement in Developing Countries' Agenda item 5 Executive Board First Regular Session, Rome 20–23 February 2006.
WFP Purchase for Progress (P4P) http://www1.wfp.org/purchase-for-progress.
WFP (2014): 'P4P Final Consolidated Procurement Report (September 2008–December 2013)'.
World Fair Trade Organization: '10 principles of Fair Trade', http://www.wfto.com/index.php?option=com_content&task=view&id=2&Itemid=14 2014.
World Bank: 'Reducing Poverty Through Sustained Equitable Growth Poverty Assessment', Report No. 29743-BUR Burkina Faso, 2005.
World Bank: 'Agriculture and Rural Development', 2015a.
World Bank Food Security https://www.worldbank.org/en/topic/food-security
World Bank on poverty line http://povertydata.worldbank.org/poverty/home/.
World Bank: 'Cambodian Agriculture in Transition: Opportunities and Risks, Economic and Sector Work', Report No. 96308-KH, May 19, 2015b.
World Union Confederation 'Scandal: Inside the global supply chains of 50 top companies' https://www.ituc-csi.org/IMG/pdf/pdffrontlines_scandal_en-2.pdf
Wright, Jonathan B.: 'Ethics in Economics', Stanford University Press 2015.
Ximena Del Carpio and Ha Minh Nguyen : 'The Unintended Consequences of Increases in the Minimum Wage', World Bank |April 25, 2012, https://blogs.worldbank.org/allaboutfinance/the-unintended-consequences-of-increases-in-the-minimum-wage.
Zobbe, Henrik: 'The Economic and Historical Foundation of the Common Agricultural Policy in Europe', Fourth European Historical Economics Society Conference, September 2001. Merton College, Oxford, UK.

Index[1]

[1] Note: Page numbers followed by 'n' refer to notes.

R. Bronkhorst, *The Economics of Human Rights*,
https://doi.org/10.1007/978-3-030-59166-3

The manufacturer's authorised representative in the EU is Springer Nature Customer Service Centre GmbH, Europaplatz 3, 69115 Heidelberg, Germany. If you have any concerns regarding our products, please contact ProductSafety@springernature.com

Printed and bound by CPI Group (UK) Ltd, Croydon, CR0 4YY

30/09/2026

02225702-0002